Christianity in China

Zhu Chengming

CHINA INTERCONTINENTAL PRESS

TABLE OF CONTENTS

Chapter 3. The Independence Movement and Localization Movement of the Christian Churches in China

Chapter 4. Three-self Patriotic Movement of the Chinese Churches

Chapter 5. Chinese Churches During the Period of Reform and Opening up to the Outside World

FOREWORD

Christianity, evolving out of existing Judaism, is based on the teachings of Jesus Christ at the height of the Roman Empire some two thousand years ago. It has developed into three major branches: Catholicism, Eastern Orthodox Church and Protestantism. What Chinese Christianity means in this book is related to the history of the dissemination and development of the Protestant faith in China.

Protestantism was the result of European religious reform in the 16th century when the German Martin Luther vehemently denounced claim of absolute divine power made by the Catholic Church and openly broke with the Vatican in Rome. Consequently, Protestantism emerged from the fetters of Catholicism and came into separate existence. From the 18th century, with the capitalist countries starting to establish overseas markets and strengthening their colonial rule, Christianity launched a worldwide missionary campaign. All the religious groups began to set up their own missions and sent missionaries abroad to conduct proselytizing activities. The overseas Christian forces grew accordingly.

The history of Chinese Protestantism began in September 1807 when an English missionary named Morrison came to China. In the early years, through force and unequal treaties, the Christian Churches grasped the 'privilege' of doing missionary work in the country. However, it repeatedly met with resistance from the Chinese people as well as government officials, and the political and cultural clashes meant the missionary work proceeded slowly. After the 20th century, thanks to the missionaries' efforts in disseminating Western culture in education, medicine, publication and other fields, the influence of Protestantism gradually spread in China. However, the relationship between the missionaries and imperialism, their arrogance and the superior attitude of Western culture still conflicted with the anti-imperialist struggle of the Chinese people time and time again, which encouraged patriotic Chinese

Christians to reconsider Christianity's social status in their country. They launched a self-independence movement and started to explore ways leading to localization of the Chinese Christian Churches.

After the founding of the People's Republic of China in 1949, Christianity underwent the transformation of the three-self patriotic movement, severed its ties with imperialism, realized self-rule, self-reliance and self-development, united the broad mass of believers, and became a patriotic religious organization.

Since China adopted the policy of reform and opening up to the outside world in 1978, Christianity has developed greatly in China. At present, there are 16 million believers throughout the country. They attach great importance to behaving themselves on different occasions and acting as the witnesses of the God's goodness. Chinese Christianity has played an active role in many respects, such as running churches under the three-self principle, fostering young priests, promptly promoting theology, carrying out social service activities, and strengthening friendly exchanges with other Christian Churches around the world. All these motives have greatly improved the image of Christianity.

It has been nearly 200 years since Christianity started spreading in China. Its evolvement and development have endured a rugged and arduous course. What is reflected in this book is only a brief overview of this course, which aims to help people better understand the path Christianity has followed, as well as its development and influence in China at present.

CHAPTER 1
EARLY MISSIONARY ACTIVITIES IN CHINA

In Chinese history, the opium war in 1840 was a turning point. After it, China's door was forced open and China moved from being an introverted feudal society to a semi-feudal, semi-colonial society. The Western Christian missionaries who had been barred when they first attempted to enter China, took advantage of this opportunity to gain the privilege of entering China freely. They started their undertakings, namely carrying out missionary activities in China.

1. Missionaries Coming to China in Early Times

Since the British missionary Morrison came to China in 1807, Christianity had started knocking at China's door. At that time, the then Chinese Qing government adopted a closed-door policy and had not yet lifted its ban on missionary activities by foreign priests issued after the Chinese Rites Controversy. Therefore, foreign missionaries could not enter China legally and could only stay in places like Hong Kong, Macao, Guangzhou, and Southeast Asia, actively preparing for their entry into China.

R. Morrison (1782-1834), sent by the London Missionary Society, was the first foreign missionary coming to china .He boarded a commercial ship from the U.S. in 1807 and reached Macao on 4th September after a four-month voyage. Three days later, he entered Guangzhou. To acquire the legal right of residence in Macao and Guangzhou, Morrison disguised his identity as a missionary for a long time and worked as a translator in the East India Company monopolized by the English merchants. When studying Chinese, he was also translating the Bible and compiling a Chinese-English Dictionary. Because of the great difficulties of penetrating the Chinese hinterland, in 1813, Morrison suggested to the London Missionary Society that an 'Outer Heng River Church' should be formed covering the territories east of India. He also put forward 'The Plan of the Outer Heng River Church' that was related to such contents as setting up schools, delivering publications, preaching together with missionaries from other Churches, etc. At that time, Morrison spent part of his time in Guangzhou dealing with the business of the East India Company, and the rest of time translating the Bible and preaching. He used the Strait of Malacca colony on the Malayan Peninsula as the base to carry out his missionary activities and mainly preached among Chinese in Macao and Southeast Asia. He also preached at his home in Guangzhou. Morrison secretly admitted the first

◎ Morrison was the first western missionary coming to China. He was translating Bible with his Chinese assistant Liang Fa.

Chinese Christian, Cai Gao, in 1814 and the first Chinese priest, Liang Fa, in 1823. As a part of 'The Plan of Outer Heng River Church', the Ying Hua School was established in Malacca in 1818 through Morrison's initiative and efforts. This, on the one hand taught Chinese to those Europeans going to China, while, on the other hand, teaching English to the local Chinese population. The London Mission Society established several Chinese periodicals in Southeast Asia. During his stay in China, Morrison was appointed the interpreter of the then special envoy of the British government, and attended the negotiations between the British government and the Qing government. Although the one-year negotiations did not achieve any result, Morrison took this opportunity of going north to get acquainted with the situation of inland China. His work won high praise from the British government, and he was designated secretary and interpreter of the first British commercial supervisor stationed in China. Later, J.R. Morrison and M.C. Morrison, his two sons, also lived in China. One of them took part in the talks on the China-Britain Nanjing Treaty and was later a member of legislative committee of the British colonial government in Hong Kong; the other was once British consul to Guangzhou.

Morrison wrote many missionary brochures, especially

Bible-the New Testament translated in 1813 and Bible-the Old Testament translated in 1819 with the help of Milne. He entitled these two translations Divine Heaven and Holy Book.

The first American missionary to China was E.C. Bridgman (1801-1861), who came on behalf of the Congregational Churches. After he arrived in Guangzhou in 1830, he lived in the American commercial residence and started to study Chinese with the help of Morrison and Liang Fa. The work Bridgman did was mainly concerned with translation, publication and education. He established the English version of China Cong News, introducing China's politics, history, people and culture to the Western world. He also translated books on history and geography like Records of the U.S.A., introducing Western culture and technology to China. After the opium war, the U.S. government sent a special envoy to China and compelled the Qing government to sign the China-U.S. Xiamen Treaty. Bridgman acted as the secretary and interpreter for the U.S. delegation and attended the signing of this unequal treaty. After that, he moved to Shanghai and became the first president of the Shanghai Arts and Science Association, which set up a library and a museum in Shanghai with the library becoming well known throughout the Far East for its large book collection. In 1861, Bridgman died of diarrhea in Shanghai.

The German missionary K.F.A. Gutzlaff (or Charles Gutzlaff, 1803-1851) arrived in Java (now part of Indonesia) in 1827. He studied the Minnan dialect (a local dialect used in Fujian Province, southeast China) and Cantonese from the local overseas Chinese, and learned some medical knowledge when he preached in hospitals. In 1829, he went to Malacca and assisted the London Missionary Society with its missionary work there. He went to Guangzhou in 1831 and acted as a translator for East India Company. Gutzlaff translated some books of the Bible and some brochures for preaching, and wrote books about the culture both of east and west, for instance, A Brief Introduction on the History of China, An Open China, and History of the U.K., etc. His most famous work was a magazine entitled Eastern and Western Oceans Monthly. In 1844, he sponsored an organization named Han Hui (or Fu Han Hui), which had more than one thousand members at its peak. Though he did much in spreading Christianity and culture, he was more interested in China's political, economic and military affairs and had helped the colonialist aggression by spying on Chinese coastal cities via cargo ships or the East India Company's scouting vessels many times. The first such occasion was in 1831. Disguised as a Chinese sailor, and carrying with him charts, mapping equipment and preaching books, he boarded a cargo ship trafficking in opium and went north along the coast. He passed through Xiamen, Taiwan, Ningbo and Shanghai and reached Tianjin in north China. In February 1832, he retraced his steps and reached not only Korea and Japan, but also places like Wusong and Baoshan that are deep inside the Yangtze River. After he returned, he wrote: 'I have made everything clear, and only hope the merchants and missionaries could pay adequate attention to these profitable places'. The third time that he went north was in October 1832, when he went directly to Fengtian (a province at that time) in northeast China through a smuggling boat offered by an opium trader. This time he did not return to Macao until April of the next year. Later, Gutzlaff published a book named The Three Voyages along China's Coast from 1831 to 1833. In fact, his scouting activities along China's coast numbered as many as ten. He himself even joined the aggressive opium war in 1840 by acting as a translator and guide for the commander of the British army.

In this period, the missionaries coming to China also included W. Milne, W.H. Medhurst and W. Lockhart from the London Missionary Society, S.W. Williams and Peter Parker from the American Congregational Church, and W.J. Boone from the American Anglican Churches, etc.

2. Entrance of the Foreign Missions into China

After the opium war, the number of missionaries sent to China by foreign missions from Britain or the U.S. started to increase. Foreign missions began to enter China to carry out their missionary activities. They included:

THE LONDON MISSIONARY SOCIETY

The London Missionary Society is the earliest church body sending missionaries to China. Besides Morrison, it sent Medhurst and Lockhart, etc to China in 1843. They rented civil residences in Shanghai in the next year and conducted missionary activities while providing medical services. Owing to the importance of Shanghai, the Church allocated money for them to purchase land and build houses there, so that an area full of churches, clinics, printing houses, and missionaries' residences evolved over time. In the following decades, The London Missionary Society had successively sent W. Muirhead, A. Wylie, A. Williamson and other missionaries to China. Besides

Shanghai, they also went to Beijing, Yantai, Hankou, Xiamen and other cities of China to carry out their missionary activities.

THE CHURCH OF ENGLAND

In 1844, the Church of England sent G. Smith and T. McClatchie to investigate in China, who set Ningbo as the center of activities. It dispatched many other missionaries to China after the second Opium War, and spread from Ningbo to Shaoxing, Hangzhou and other places with its preaching area covering about half of Zhejiang Province. It also established the Holy Trinity Church in Shanghai, the Holy Trinity School in Ningbo, as well as Ying Hua School and some drug addicts' treatment institutions.

THE BRITISH BAPTIST CHURCH

The British Baptist Church sent two missionaries to China's Shandong Province in 1859 and established its base in Yantai. However, little was achieved. In 1869, the famous missionary Timothy Richard went to Yantai and opened up a new prospect for its missionary activities.

THE AMERICAN CONGREGATIONAL CHURCH

In 1843, the American Congregational Church for the first

time sent its missionary D. Ball to Hong Kong to practice medicine as well as carry out missionary work. He went to Guangzhou two years later. It was this church to which Sun Yat-sen, leader of China's modern democratic revolution was admitted when he became a Christian believer. After 1847, the church sent many missionaries to preach in Fuzhou. They established a school there in 1853, which was the predecessor of the

◎ On 25th June 1986, a choir was praying for peace in the Chongwenmen Church in Beijing.

Fuzhou Concord University. In 1860, when the second Opium War broke out, H. Blodget went north to Tianjin with the British army and reached Beijing four years later, establishing a church presence in north China. He established the famous Dengshikou Church. After 1865, A.H. Smith, D.Z.Sheffield and other missionaries went to north China successively. The former later wrote works like Rural Lives in China, China in Changes and

Disturbances, and became an expert on Chinese issues, while the latter became the first president of North China Concord University.

AMERICAN ANGLICAN (EPISCOPALIAN) CHURCH

The American Anglican Church dispatched Bishop Boone to Shanghai in 1844. He bought land on the north bank of the Suzhou River (later Creek) on which he built churches and schools. Later, the church extended its development towards the Yangtze Delta. After the third bishop S.I.J. Shereschewsky took office in 1877, the church dedicated itself to running schools and translating books. It established the St. John's School that evolved into the St. John's University later on.

NORTHERN AND SOUTHERN BAPTIST CHURCH

In 1845, the American Northern and Southern Baptist Church began missionary activities in southern China. Based on Shanghai, it developed towards eastern China from 1847. One of its missionaries in Shanghai, whose name was T. Yates, had frequent contacts with the Small Sword Association in the 1850s when that association began an armed uprising. He sent the information he had gathered about the association to the U.S.

consulate and published it in the North China Victory News. The information was later compiled and published in the book Taiping Army. The Northern and Southern Baptists usually operated in areas south to the Yangtze River, such as Ningbo, Hangzhou and Shanghai.

AMERICAN PRESBYTERIAN CHURCH

The American Presbyterian Church started its missionary activities in Guangdong Province, Xiamen and Ningbo in 1844, and gradually moved on to Shanghai and Shandong Province. By 1877, the number of its Chinese believers totaled more than 1,100. It established the newspaper titled Tong Wen Bao. Famous missionaries in the early 20th century like J.L. Stuart and F.W. Price were from this Church.

AMERICAN WESLEYANS

In 1847, The American Wesleyan Society started its missionary work in Fuzhou where one of its missionaries named S.L. Baldwin established a magazine entitled Missionary Work, which was the first magazine intended for the foreign missionaries in China to exchange their ideas. The famous missionary Y.J. Allen, another Wesleyan, was once director of the China

Methodist Episcopal Church after he came to China in 1860.

THE CHINESE HOME MISSIONARY SOCIETY

The Chinese Home Missionary Society was established in 1865 by an English missionary named J.H. Taylor. It was a transnational and trans-church religious group. It required the missionaries to try to live and dress in the Chinese way and preach in the spirit of sacrifice without compensation. Its headquarters was in Shanghai, while its policy of development was to avoid the coastal cities where the big churches conducted their missionary activities and to operate in the Chinese hinterland. It enjoyed some development in provinces like Sichuan, Henan, Shanxi and Yunnan. By the early 20th century, The Chinese Home Missionary Society had set up some 700 churches and many primary schools and hospitals, with more than 19,000 believers.

3. Features of Early Missionary Activities

In the early years since Christianity was introduced to China, it was not only restricted in various forms by the Qing government, but was also unknown to the vast majority of Chinese people. Therefore, it developed with great difficulty and achieved little progress. To break the deadlock, missionaries did not hesitate to resort to some non-religious means to facilitate their activities. The main features of their work during this period were as follows:

1) WITH THE SHARED GOAL OF FORCING CHINA'S DOOR OPEN, MISSIONARIES, BUSINESSMEN AND DIPLOMATS JOINED HANDS TO CARRY OUT INVASIVE ACTIVITIES.

To force China's door open, missionaries were doing missionary work for the churches on the one hand and serving the cause of the colonialist invasion on the other. They bore many responsibilities and played different roles on different occasions. For example, as already noted, Charles Gutzlaff, the German

14

missionary, had dressed like a sailor and gone to north China to scout for information many times, and when the Opium War began, he simply devoted himself to working as the interpreter and guide for the commander of the British invading army. In the spring of 1842, when the British army occupied Ningbo and Zhoushan, he was appointed governor of the local administration. He went to Shanghai soon after the British army seized it. On behalf of the British army, he issued notices to reassure the public and extorted as much as 300,000 taels of silver from the then Shanghai governor for redemption of the city. In June of that year, he took part in the seizure of Zhenjiang after the invaders had previously failed many times in their attacks. In the peace talks between the British government and the Qing government, he participated in the drafting and signing of the unequal Nanjing Treaty. In the next year, he acted as translator when China and the U.S. signed their first unequal treaty-the Xiamen Treaty. Many American missionaries who came to China in the 1830s, like Bridgman and Parker, also published their remarks preaching the use of force and advocating an aggressive war. At the end of 1834, when diplomatic relations between China and Britain collapsed, all English businessmen in Guangzhou petitioned the British King to send troops to China to threaten the Qing

◎ A new church in Shantou City of Guangdong Province.

government to open up Ningbo and Xiamen as trade ports. At that time, Bridgman wrote articles repeatedly in the China Cong News to express his support for their petitions. He said: 'If all countries fail in persuading China, then it should be forced to take our rights and interests as its duty'. In his words, the opening of China's door to the invaders had become a duty of China and a right of foreign countries! He also said: 'As far as China's attitude is concerned, no government can treat it politely without the use of force'. One year later, the confrontation between the two countries was even tenser. An article entitled Signing Treaties with China - An Urgent and Important Requirement was published in China Cong News, clearly proposing to forcibly compel China to sign treaties. In the notes added to the article, Bridgman said China was a weak country with vast lands and a regiment of British army could defeat several provinces' Chinese troops. So, guns should be used to back up negotiation. After the outbreak of the Opium War, he wrote about the war as well as the political negotiation, flagrantly announcing that 'the time is up and China must give in or be conquered.' Another missionary named David Abeel who came to China along with Bridgman also trumpeted that war was 'the God's means to prize China's door open'. Nevins, who was from the North American Presbyterian Church and who had reached China in 1854, also made it clear that 'no matter if this war is just or not, it is endorsed by God to open a new epoch for our relationship with China'. Parker, an American missionary and doctor, also served the U.S. government cordially. When the war broke out, he was in the U.S. on leave. He launched a series of political activities and submitted to the U.S. State Department a report on the situation in China, recommending the U.S. government to take advantage of the conflicts between China and Britain. He thought it was a golden opportunity for the U.S. to get involved, and 'Chinese people's trust on the U.S. probably exceed their trust on other countries'. His report drew the close attention of the U.S. Secretary of State, who promptly sent him to Britain and France to find out their true intentions regarding China. In December 1842, the Nanjing Treaty between China and Britain was already signed and five ports including Guangzhou had been forced open. Knowing the contents of the treaty, the U.S. government quickly sent a delegation headed by Gu Sheng to China and claimed to sign a treaty with China. Gu Sheng appointed Bridgman and Parker as secretaries to the delegation. After the Xiamen Treaty was signed, Parker totally abandoned his missionary work and wholeheartedly engaged himself in diplomatic and political activities for over ten years. At the beginning, he was designated secretary to the U.S. special envoy to China, and was then promoted to charge d'affaires in 1847. He was formally appointed plenipotentiary in August 1855 by the U.S. president, who let him present his credentials to the emperor of China. Before he went to Guangzhou to assume his new post, he visited the British and French diplomatic compounds to discuss the situation. After he reached Guangzhou, he continued his talks with the British and French deputies and concluded that the use of force should be maintained to back up their talks with China.

2) MISSIONARY ACTIVITIES WERE CARRIED OUT THROUGH PRACTICING MEDICINE AND RUNNING SCHOOLS.

Practicing medicine and running schools was a key approach to disseminating Western civilization. In early times, missionaries spent most of their energy gaining a solid foothold for preaching in China. The reason why they began practicing medicine was because they wanted to break their estrangement with and close the distance between themselves and the Chinese people, and to win the people's trust and favor. An American Christian scholar named Latourette considered that there were two functions of preaching through practicing medicine: one was to convince the Chinese of the value of the Western medicine; the other was to remove Chinese people's prejudice against Christianity. Parker was the first missionary doctor in China. He set up a clinic and successfully cured many patients' eye problems, sometimes even by surgery. His work got the 'magic' of Western medicine across to the Chinese people and greatly enhanced the missionaries' reputation in China. In Shanghai, Lockhart and Medhurst established a clinic at the southern gate of the city at the end of 1843, and treated as many as 10,000 patients in two years. After the second Opium War, the missionaries established many hospitals in China's hinterland, including Shanghai Ren Ji

Hospital (1861), West Gate Women and Children's Hospital (1885), Shantou Fu Yin Hospital (1867), Hangzhou Guang Ji Hospital (1880), etc. These hospitals absorbed far more believers than the churches did and greatly promoted the religious work.

However, practicing medicine required professional knowledge and training and could only be exercised by a small number of missionaries, which made the choice of running schools more common among missionaries. At the very beginning, some missionary couples just set up very simple and shabby houses to teach children about the Bible as well as basic arts and science. In order to appeal to the children, they also provided free lunches and snacks or even money in compensation for the time when they neglected housework in favor of study. With the increasingly strengthened ability in doing missionary work, all Churches supported their missionaries to build upgraded and specialized schools, like Xin Yi School in Ningbo, Pei Ya School and Du En School in Shanghai, Wen Shan Women's School in Fuzhou, etc. According to statistics in the 1870s, there were about 350 schools run by missionaries with approximately 6,000 students. After that, the scale of the schools continuously expanded and they were run in an increasingly standardized manner. In the late 19th century, the famous schools in China included: Dengzhou Arts Association in Shandong, Lu He Middle School in Hebei, St. John's School and Zhong Xi School in Shanghai, etc. The schools established by the missionaries pursued Western teaching principles and curricula. While spreading Christian ideas they had also taught modern science and arts, so that they admitted a lot of Christians on the one hand and cultivated many intellectuals on the other.

3) DRAWING CHINESE PEOPLE'S INTEREST IN CHRISTIANITY BY DISSEMINATING WESTERN MODERN SCIENCE.

From the time missionaries first came to China, they attached great importance to disseminating Christianity by preaching in letters and words. The early missionaries like Morrison and his sons, Milne, Medhurst, Gutzlaff and Bridgman, had all translated the Bible into Chinese. In order to achieve concerted and coordinated translation, the British and American missionaries established a Committee for Bible Translation in 1843 and published the Chinese version of New Testament and Old Testament successively in 1859 and 1862. Nevertheless, it was far from enough to carry out missionary activities with only a translation of the Bible. All missionaries engaged in introducing the cultural outlook of the West to the Chinese people through books and reading materials or even articles and brochures written by themselves. The early missionaries wrote many books and brochures introducing Western knowledge, for instance, the history, geography, politics and economies of various countries, etc. Observation on Secularity Monthly, established by Morrison and Milne in Malacca in 1815 and distributed to the local overseas Chinese for free, on the one hand briefly presented the heliocentric theory and knowledge about solar and lunar eclipses; on the other hand, it attribute all theories to the power of God. In 1823, Medhurst established Selected Important News Monthly that carried articles on religion, current events, history, geography and common knowledge, etc. From 1828 to 1829, Medhurst started World News, the first type monthly in Chinese. It was published in Malacca and carried articles of news, history, and religion, etc. Gutzlaff established a periodical titled Eastern and Western Oceans Monthly between 1833 and 1838 and contributed many articles on the culture and people of other countries. To extend their influence, many Churches established specialized publishing houses among which Mo Hai Book House by London Missionary Society, Mei Hua Printing House and Yi Zhi Book Association by the Presbyterian Church were relatively famous.

Besides propaganda materials of Christianity, these publishing houses also published many books about science. Chinese people's earliest knowledge about algebra, geometry, physics, astronomy and geography came from these publications.

. . . .

4. Resistance of the Chinese People-Missionary Cases Occurred Repeatedly

From the 1860s, with a series of unequal treaties that defined 'tolerance in treating missionaries', the Christian churches had entered China with a legal identity. In the next 30 to 40 years, their activities marched into a new phase of development. However, contrary to what the missionaries had expected, the spread and development of Christianity in China still met with all kinds of misunderstandings, obstructions and resistance from the Chinese people.

The missionaries entered China along with the colonialist powers. The privileges laid down by the unequal treaties often led to their boldness, fearlessness and violence towards the Chinese people, which sparked the discontent and resistance from rural farmers and urban civilians, and sometimes even nobles and low-ranking officials. Since the 1860s, anti-Christian missionary cases had occurred all over the country. The following are some of these cases:

QINGPU MISSIONARY CASE

This was the first missionary case to occur since Christianity was introduced into China. In March 1843, three missionaries from the London Missionary Society in Shanghai violated the local regulations by distributing gospel tracts in Qingpu County, Jiangsu Province. Tens of thousands of local people and sailors crowded to watch the foreigners whom they had never seen before. The missionaries wielded sticks, hitting and injuring some people, which aroused the outrage of the crowd and led to a conflict. The county governor hurried to escort the missionaries back to Shanghai. The Shanghai governor promised to arrest the 'criminals', however, the British consul in Shanghai took it as an excuse to repudiate tariffs, blockade the local sailors' grain ships, and even deploy troops to intimidate the governor of Liangjiang (an upper provincial level official to whom the aforementioned two governors were responsible at that time) based in Nanjing. As a result, the two local governors were discharged and prosecuted, 10 villagers were punished, and the missionaries got 300 taels of silver for compensation.

TAIWAN FENGSHAN MISSIONARY CASE

In September 1868, some villagers in Fengshan (Taiwan

Province) were bullied by a Christian named Zhuang Qingfeng, resulting in local people burning several local churches and driving out the British missionaries. The British merchants who monopolized the camphor industry in Taiwan soon came to rescue with weapons. The British government, on the pretext of protecting the merchants, even sent warships to Taiwan and bombarded Anping County, killing the general of the local garrison, burning the barracks and arsenal. The Governor of Minzhe (an upper provincial level official who was in charge of the Taiwan affairs at that time) was forced to negotiate. Consequently, he dismissed some local officials and paid indemnities to the British. Besides, the Qing government was compelled to give up the franchise of camphor previously belonging to a state-owned factory in Taiwan.

YANGZHOU MISSIONARY CASE

Relying on the British colonist forces, James Hudson Taylor, a missionary from the Chinese Home Missionary Society, coercively rented a civilian house for preaching in Yangzhou, Jiangsu Province in August 1868, and was vehemently opposed by the local people who even smashed up his residence, forcing him to run away to Zhejiang Province with his family. Being

◎ In the evening of 24 December 1984, the Chongwenmen Church in Beijing held a Christmas praying event.

informed of what had happened, the British consul in Shanghai promptly went directly to Nanjing with a warship and put pressure on Zeng Guofan, Governor of Liangjiang. Consequently, the Governor of Yangzhou was dismissed and reparations were paid to the church. Zeng Guofan even put up an announcement in front of the church for its protection. However, when news of this case reached to Britain, it stirred up the British criticism of Taylor, saying he had brought the trouble on himself and caused war. Some even requested that all British missionaries in China should be withdrawn, which reflected the fact that the British people were also against missionary wrongdoing in China.

Despite this frustration, Taylor sent people back to Yangzhou to set up a base only one year later.

CHONGQING MISSIONARY CASE

The missionary case caused by the British and American who used coercion to build churches in Chongqing in July 1886, was actually the second incident following one by the Catholics 23 years before. The American missionaries not only built Western style houses in important locations by force, but also hired gangsters to oppress the dissatisfied local people, which caused outrage. As a result, people stopped working, businessmen ceased doing business, and examinees refused to take their exams. Over 3,000 people burned three houses belonging to the missionaries, as well as 250 houses of Christian believers. They then went on to destroy the British consulate when supporters of the churches fired on them and killed some people. The result of this case was the British and U.S. consuls asking the Qing government for compensation of 41.57 thousand taels of silver and two Chinese were executed.

CAOZHOU MISSIONARY CASE (OR JUYE MISSIONARY CASE)

In June 1896, the struggle between the villagers and

Churches for lands in Caozhou city, Shandong Province triggered an uprising by the local branch of the Broadsword Association, who were then joined by other branches of the Broadsword Association in nearby Jimo city demanding the demolition of the churches and elimination of the foreigners. They threatened to 'extinguish Christianity and Catholicism, and drive all foreigners out of China's Central Plain'. They destroyed over 30 churches and killed two German priests. In 1897, Kaiser Wilhelm took advantage of this accident and a German army landed in Jiaozhou Bay and occupied Jiaozhou City. An alarmed Qing government eventually agreed to all the German demands. Besides punishing the perpetrators and local officials, other clauses included: 1) compensation of 3000 taels of silver for losses of the churches; 2) building one church in each of the three places (Jining, Caozhou and Juye) with each church costing 66 thousand taels of silver; 3) a law to protect German missionaries in China. The China-Germany Jiao Ao Concession Treaty was signed, defining that the whole area of Jiaozhou Bay was leased to Germany, which was entitled to build the Jiao Ji Railway and to explore for minerals in a strip 15 km wide on both sides of the line. As a result, China not only lost Jiaozhou Bay, but also gradually yielded the whole Shandong Province into the hands of German forces. The Caozhou case had also demonstrated that the integration of the foreign missionary forces with foreign aggression and expansion had evolved to a new stage.

YI HE TUAN MOVEMENT

In 1900, the Yi He Tuan (Boxer) Movement broke out in China, which shocked the world. It was an anti-imperialism patriotic movement launched mainly by peasants in which the confrontation between Christianity and the Chinese people over the previous half century reached its peak. The Yi He Tuan, Broadsword Association and Mei Hua Quan were originally secret martial arts clubs in north China. At the beginning, Yi He Tuan raised the banner of 'overturning Qing Dynasty and supporting the Ming Dynasty' and 'resisting the government and eliminating violence'. Later on, it gradually involved itself into an anti-foreign movement, especially the churches. It was supported by some diehards in the Qing government who relied on Yi He Tuan to realize their goal of defeating the foreigners and saving the Qing Dynasty.

In June 1900, Yi He Tuan marched from Shandong Province to Beijing, burned the racetrack and villas of the British Embassy, and besieged all foreign churches and diplomatic compounds in the capital. The Christian missionaries motivated five to six thousand believers to build defensive works around their compounds and to fight with their soldiers. Many of these

◎ In the late June 1988, a grand consecration ceremony was held in Shanghai Mu En Church that has a history of one hundred years. In this ceremony, the 74-year old Sun Yanli and 60-year old Shen Yifan was promoted bishop. This was the first time in 33 years for the Chinese Christian Churches to celebrate the consecration ceremony for new bishop.

believers died unfortunately. The Yi He Tuan, together with the army of the Qing government besieged the diplomatic compounds and two churches for 56 days until 14th August when the eight-power allied forces captured Beijing. Almost at the same time,

Yi He Tuan's branch in Tianjin raised the banner of 'Supporting the Qing Dynasty and Eliminating Foreigners'. They burned three churches on 14th June and one more the next day. The government gave them great encouragement, and even the governor's office building was used as their headquarters. Many Christians ran to the Zizhulin Concession for refuge, and while some barricaded themselves in the churches. They would be severely punished if captured, possibly beheaded. Yi He Tuan in Zhili Province, headed by a woman boxer named Zhu Hongdeng, attracted many civilian recruits. It kept its momentum of development unchecked by 'destroying railways, burning churches and killing foreign priests'. Especially in Baoding, when the local people got to know that the eight-power allied forces had conquered Dagukou (a military base defending Tianjin), they were so angry that they burned several churches and killed many foreign missionaries. Six American and British priests asked the army of the Qing government for help, but the army feared the power of Yi He Tuan and turned the foreigners over to the insurgents for execution. This movement even spread to such remote areas as Inner Mongolia and northeast China. Foreigners were killed when captured, and those Chinese Christians who did not abandon their religious belief or even spoke up for it were also killed.

Surrounded by the national exclusive sentiment of the Chinese people, Western religions became the biggest target for attack.

Statistics in The History of Chinese Christianity by Wang Zhixin showed that during the Yi He Tuan movement, 53 Catholic missionaries and 188 Protestant missionaries were killed.

To oppress the Yi He Tuan movement, the imperial powers directly resorted to the use of armed force. Britain, U.S., Germany, Italy, Russia, Austria, Japan and France formed the eight-power allied forces to intimidate the Qing government into suppressing the movement. They committed untold crimes on Chinese territory by burning, killing and robbing at will. In the middle of July 1900, the eight-power allied forces captured Tianjin, and on 14th August Beijing was occupied. On 9th Sept. 1901, the Qing government was compelled to sign the humiliating Xinchou Treaty and to pay 450 million taels of silver as war reparations. With that, China became 'a semi-colonial country under the joint mandate of the imperial powers'. Even during the process of invasion by the eight powers, the missionaries played a disgraceful role. Many of them became guides and accompanied the invaders as military padres, attended the looting of Beijing and presented suggestions and proposals for the dismemberment of China.

CHAPTER 2
CLIMAX OF MISSIONARY ACTIVITIES AND REVITALIZATION OF THE CHRISTIAN CHURCHES IN THE EARLY 20TH CENTURY

1. China's Opening to the Outside World and Social Changes

The Yi He Tuan Movement was crushed by the eight-power allied forces, which invaded China and forced the Qing government to sign the unequal Xinchou Treaty in 1901. Before the treaty was signed, the Western powers clinched an agreement on the U.S. proposal that although they would not raise demands for land concessions, China must practice an open-door policy to guarantee their interests in China. The Qing government acceded to their request in exchange for the maintenance of its rule over the country. Although the Xinchou Treaty did not

◎ In the Christmas Eve of 1992, a candlelight-praying event was held in the Chongwenmen Church. The choir of the church was singing.

include any claim for land concessions and China was still an independent and unified country in the formal sense, as a matter of fact, the aggressive powers had obtained the right to garrison, the right of political control and the right of economic exploitation, leaving China no more than a semi-colonial country under the mandate of the powers.

In addition to huge reparations as well as social and diplomatic privileges, to prevent the Chinese people's resistance movements similar to Yi He Tuan from happening again, the aggressive powers specially defined in the Xinchou Treaty that 'the Chinese people are for ever forbidden to establish or join any anti-imperialism organization. All perpetrators will be executed. The local officials are responsible for banning such activities, and those who fail the work will be dismissed.' This regulation paved the way for the development of Christianity in China. With a strong political and economic backup, as well as the protection from the Qing governments at both central and local levels, the missionaries could freely enter China's hinterland unchecked, putting aside their worries about resistance and opposition.

All these developments brought great losses to China and made the Chinese people understand that, when facing the impact of the Western civilization, blind arrogance and refusal to change would only lead to defeat, neither could such backward means as superstition, martial arts or an exclusivist attitude to gain victory. The sole way out was to change and reform. Some people began to turn their attention to the ills of society and search for an effective therapy for social reform. The anti-religion mood among the Chinese people had not dimmed, but they adopted a different approach than before. People did not simply reject all foreign cultures, but sought to absorb the advanced and scientific parts in order to promote national development. After the Yi He Tuan Movement was defeated, the conservative forces in the Qing

聖誕音樂會

◎ On an Christmas music evening held on 15 December 1987, Bai Yansheng, Bai Rongsheng and Bai Wensheng, three brothers in a mouth organ team of Beijing Young Men's Christian Association, brought the 5-day-long religious artistic event to an end by an ensemble of mouth organs. This event, which was organized by Beijing Young Men's Christian Association, also included activities like literature lectures and music appreciation.

government received a heavy blow, while the advocates of Westernization gained some concrete power. They tried to imitate the Western modernization process and seek a new way out by practicing new policies and establishing a modern constitution. The revolution never ended despite many failures. The capitalist democrats headed by Sun Yat-sen continued to resort to revolution to change society. The American missionary F. Rawlinson, when summarizing the obvious revolutionary trend in China in the 20 years after 1900, pointed out: 'This revolutionary trend did not aim at reforming old ideas or removing some people in power, but at replacing all old principles and systems with new ones.'

Of all the changes at the beginning of the 20th century, the Xin Hai Revolution in 1911 was one that caused the deepest social changes. It overturned the corrupted feudal imperialism and founded a new democratic republic country. It was not simply a replacement of the old regime by a new one, but the complete burial of the old system. On 1st Jan. 1912, Sun Yat-sen, was sworn in as provisional president of the Republic of China in Nanjing. Soon afterwards he announced The Proclamation of Provisional President and A Letter to All Compatriots, expressing his determination to 'eliminate the toxin of dictatorship and establish the republic system to achieve the objectives of the revolution'. The Provisional Law of the Republic of China promulgated on Mar. 11 clearly stipulated that 'all people are equal and there is no discrimination in races, classes and religions', 'people have the freedom of person, residence, possessions, speech, the press, assembly, association and religious belief', and the legal rights of Christianity were protected. In handling the relationship between the state and religion, the new government pursued the model of 'separation of religion from politics' advocated by Western countries: all religions are equal; religion does not interfere in political affairs; and, the State protects the freedom of belief. The improvement of the relationship between the State and the churches laid a solid social foundation for the development of Christianity in China. Later, despite the attempts by Yuan Shikai, who usurped power to set up Confucianism as the state religion, but failed due to the opposition of all Chinese people and religious groups, the idea of separation of religion from politics and freedom in religious belief had been well received by the majority of Chinese people and had become a symbol of modern society.

2. Change in the Means of Christian Missionary Activities

To the Christian churches, the large-scale bloodshed seen in the uprising of the Yi He Tuan Movement not only frustrated them, but also was a wake-up call. Considering the grave lessons, many missionaries look at their own past wrongdoing, looking squarely at their own problems and trying to change in order to end Chinese people's discontent and rebuild the social image of Christianity.

Even Western missionaries themselves acknowledged that Christianity, protected by the unequal peace agreements and suspected to have been involved in politics, was strongly opposed by most of the Chinese people. Therefore, an American missionary called Arthur Smith pointed out: 'Christianity must gain people's acknowledgement, reverence, consent and acceptance before it can win a strong foothold in China'. He accepted that the criticism of the missionaries that they were excessively interested in politics and the indictments were 'fair' and that the Christian churches must show introspection in regard to their own actions. Talking about foreign missionaries' involvement in the eight-power allied forces' military actions, another American missionary F.L. Hawks noted: 'When responding to this accusation, at least we are afraid that the Roman Catholic missionaries have to admit their crimes. They are guilty of engaging themselves to the political affairs.' After the Yi He Tuan Movement, the British and American governments and the Christian churches themselves worked out corresponding restrictions on the interference in political and diplomatic affairs. In the light of the order of the British government, the British embassy and consulate to China issued a notice that prohibited missionaries from directly interfering in their believers' civil affairs. When interference seemed necessary, it should be carried out by the local consul. A German newspaper in Shanghai also claimed that missionaries should not be engaged in work other than introducing Christianity, otherwise they would be punished and expelled. And the missionaries themselves also came to know that some of the admitted Christians were not qualified and thus were more careful than before about getting involved in their cases. Thus, the number of conflicts between the people and the churches sharply declined and missionary cases gradually subsided.

The missionaries in China also came to know that it was necessary to reform the old ways of preaching in order to eliminate the Chinese people's hatred and exclusivist attitude towards foreigners in general and missionaries in particular. In the 19th century, most of the missionaries adhered to the traditional ways of preaching, such as teaching doctrines and distributing religious tracts, etc. In this way, the admitted believers were mainly people in the middle or lower classes of society, or even old and weak people who lived on religious relief. Therefore, Christianity obtained little social influence in spite of the increase in the number of believers. And most importantly, the intellectuals and people in the upper classes commonly held Christianity in contempt. In the early part of the 20th century, through their own experiences, some missionaries came to recognize that the expected effects could not be realized by preaching alone and the ways of spreading the faith must be changed. Some proposed to run schools and to be actively involved in the social affairs so as to reform the society and win people's hearts. Allen Young, an American missionary, was this type. He was once engaged in translating English books and teaching English. In the course of disseminating Western culture, he found it more acceptable by the Chinese people especially the intellectuals to enlighten their minds first, then transform the Chinese culture and finally proselytize them. Therefore, he was keen to carry out undertakings like education and publishing. The British missionary Timothy Richard was also a man of this type who actively engaged in activities of education, publication and disaster relief. After the Yi He Tuan Movement disappeared, some liberal missionaries recommended the U.S. government to speed up fostering pro-American intellectuals by utilizing the indemnities prescribed in the Xinchou Treaty to support more young Chinese students to study in the U.S. and to establish schools in China. In 1906, Arthur Smith reported to the then U.S. President Roosevelt on the Chinese political situation, claiming that the best way to prevent movements like Yi He Tuan from happening again was to disseminate Christianity and set up church schools, and suggesting the return of some indemnities for the Qing government to establish schools. His suggestions were appreciated by President Roosevelt. Afterwards, the U.S. government did indeed spend some part of the indemnities establishing Tsing Hua University, and Timothy Prichard utilized the indemnities to force the Shanxi government to establish Shanxi University. Meanwhile, the British and American churches stepped up the dispatch of missionaries to China to run schools, hospitals and charities. The Chinese church universities made rapid progress in both quantity and quality. They taught Western culture and science, which objectively conformed to the Chinese people's needs for reform and development. The religious teachings in these schools also helped make Christianity acceptable to some young students, leaving others, if not necessarily believing, but at least favorably disposed towards it. Consequently, Christian churches made rapid development in this period.

3. The Development of the Christian Churches

The years after 1900 saw the most dramatic development of Christianity in China. The number of foreign missions and missionaries coming to China, and the number of Chinese Christians, both enjoyed unprecedented increase.

According to statistics, there were 61 Foreign Christian Missions in 1900, and 67 in 1906. The number sharply rose to 130 in 1919, with another 36 Christian groups independently running businesses of various types. Almost all Christian Churches had sent missionaries to China; in addition, many newly formed churches mainly from the U.S. with a relatively conservative theological ideology also started to preach, such as the Seventh Day Adventists who came to China in 1901, followed soon afterwards by the Assembly of God and the Mennonite Church, who entered Fujian Province in 1911. The British Pentecostal Church arrived in Yunnan Province in 1912. Besides, some Christian international organizations or industrial organizations also sent missionaries to set up their branches in

China, for example, the Salvation Army and Christian Association of the Postal and Telecommunications Industry.

There were 1,500 foreign missionaries in China in 1900. The number increased to 3,445 in 1905 and 6,636 in 1919, up more than four times in only 20 years. From 1914 to 1918, during World War One, few missionaries came to China, but it was in this period that American missionaries outnumbered the British for the first time, accounting for 60% of the total. Thereafter, the Americans were dominant. By 1920, the foreign missionaries had set up 693 centers as well as 1,037 preaching institutions for carrying out missionary activities. Most of the missionaries stayed in the eight big cities: Shanghai, Beijing, Guangzhou, Nanjing, Fuzhou, Changsha, Chengdu and Jinan. There were over 100 missionaries in each of these cities on average, covering 26% of the total. About 57% of the missionaries were scattered in the coastal provinces, compared to 17% in the inland provinces. The missionary activities could be characterized as radiating out from the coastal areas to inland, and from the central cities to the surrounding villages.

The total number of Christians in China was 80,000 in 1900, which rose to 170,000 in 1906. This was the period that Christianity developed fastest. In 1914, the number grew to

◎ The Christians were performing songs after make-up when they celebrated Christmas in 1999.

250,000, then 360,000 in 1920. From 1900 to 1920, the total number of Christians increased 4.5 times. The Chinese Christians mainly concentrated in the coastal cities and villages, and Christians in Guangdong, Fujian, Zhejiang, Jiangsu, Shandong, Zhili and Fengtian provinces accounted for 71% of the total. Notably, there was a big increase in the number of Christians in church schools. From 1907 to 1920, the total number increased by 105%, while the number of students in church schools increased by 322%, with teachers increasing by 374%. According to statistics from the Young Men's Christian Association on 133 church schools in 1920, Christians amounted to 49% of the student body; if those who believed in Christianity but not yet admitted were included, the figure might have exceeded 50%. And the rate would be even higher if the graduates had been included. Because most of the admitted Christians came from church schools, the quality of the Christian church membership was improved. As far as the educational level was concerned, in every 75 people in the country there was only one student, while one out of three Christians was a student. Quite a number of Christians could read and write, especially in Jiangsu, Guangdong, Shandong, and Zhili provinces. The composition of the Chinese Christians changed and the social status of the Christians was enhanced. Sun Yat-sen, who led the Xin Hai Revolution, was just a believer, as were many of his colleagues, such as Chen Haodong, Chen Shaobai, etc. Among all the congressmen in the government of the Republic of China, Christians numbered as many as 60. They accounted for 65% of staff members of the Guangdong provincial government. At that time, China's ambassador to Germany, the Minister of Agriculture and Forestry, and the Vice Commander of the Navy, etc were all Christians. And many experts in education and medical science were also Christians.

With the growth of the Chinese churches, indigenous Chinese missionaries gradually emerged, especially after 1907 when more and more Chinese missionaries were accorded Christian titles. In 1906, there were altogether 345 Chinese priests, which increased to 1,065 in 1919, up approximately threefold. To foster priests, the foreign missions established many theological colleges and bible schools. According to statistics contained in a book entitled China For Christ, there had been 13 theological colleges, 48 men's and 52 women's bibles schools around the country by 1920. The theological colleges cultivated many priests, clergymen and high-level Chinese leaders for the Churches, among whom about 7% had bachelor's degrees, 25% had graduated from middle schools, and all the remainder had received some degree of education. In 1907, when the Missionary Century Conference was held, the Chinese representatives only accounted for one third of the 115 representatives. However, when the China For Christ Conference was held in 1919, Chinese representatives accounted for half of all the attendees. The Chinese church leaders had become an indispensable force in the cause of disseminating Christianity.

Besides such indirect means as establishing schools, hospitals and publishing houses, the more effective way to carry out missionary work was to preach directly to the people. Since the Republic of China was founded, the social environment of China had changed greatly. The Chinese people no longer felt strange about foreigners, especially those students who had good command of English and could communicate with foreigners directly. The missionary work conducted by the Chinese clergy had become more acceptable to the people and had achieved good results. Therefore, basic missionary work was highlighted again and became an important means to revitalize the churches.

Missionary work in academic circles was mainly organized and carried out by the Young Men's Christian Association. In 1911, it began inviting some famous American missionaries like J.R. Mott and S. Eddy many times to preach to the masses in large and medium sized cities around China. Each time, the number of attendees reached several thousand. The audiences were mainly young students and intellectuals. To cater to student tastes, they applied specific tactics by starting their speeches with scientific and philosophical problems, which made the speeches full of academic meaning. They also gave speeches on issues that were of the greatest concern of the young students at that time, such as social problems and the ways to save the country. Since their speeches attached great importance to the current situation of China and the specific characteristics of the young students, they were well received. After their preaching, some people converted to Christianity on the spot, some expressed their willingness to learn more about Christianity and some signed up for study courses.

During this period, there appeared different types of preaching associations that launched an extensive revitalization movement. In terms of location, the preaching work could be carried out in churches, villages, streets, schools or open-air grounds; in terms of time, it could last a week, a day, or be held on Lord's day, or in the Spring Festival or Christmas; in terms of formality, it could be personal preaching, family preaching or word preaching; there were also preaching activities for different walks of life, including some special groups like soldiers, rickshaw men, prisoners, etc. Missionaries from the American churches that were theologically conservative laid great stress on working people who lived at the bottom of society and whipped them into a religious frenzy through their preaching. On many occasions, the audiences became extremely excited. They cried for remission and confessed their sins. Many in the audience were converted to Christianity. After they repented, these people were even more warmhearted in doing their missionary work and leading people around them to believe in Christianity. The cause of Christianity saw great development.

CHAPTER 3
THE INDEPENDENCE MOVEMENT AND LOCALIZATION MOVEMENT OF THE CHRISTIAN CHURCHES IN CHINA

1. The Independence Movement Aiming at Shaking Off Control of the Foreign Missions

The self-independent churches mainly referred to those established and run independently by Chinese clergymen, which had already got rid of foreign mission control in organization and rejected their financial support. Owing to the restrictions imposed by the specific historical conditions, the Chinese Christians had always been caught in a low status with no power in the churches. However, in the mid-19th century, there had been some examples of Chinese Christians trying to establish independent churches.

◎ On 21 November 1992, the choir of Guangzhou Young Women's Christian Association performed to celebrate the 80th anniversary of the association's founding. Guangzhou Young Women's Christian Association is mainly dedicated to social services.

Chen Mengnan, a scholar in Guangzhou, who had admired Christianity for quite a long time after he made a self-study of it, had hesitated to be baptized and gain admittance to the church, because according to the rules, there must be a priest touching his head while praying before he could be admitted. He thought that he was a noble Chinese scholar, and how could he be baptized by a foreigner? Later, he heard there was a Chinese priest in Zhaoqing. Then, he spent many days getting there to ask this Chinese priest to baptize him. After baptism, he thought since

Christianity was the rule of God, the latter would be a foreigner in foreign countries but a Chinese in China. That was to say, a foreign God only belonged to foreigners and there must be a God of the Chinese; therefore, Chinese Christians naturally should establish their own churches and do missionary work by themselves. In 1872, he rented a house to set up a Church with the help of some Christians in Guangzhou as well as overseas Chinese. The next year, he established a totally Chinese run Missionary Association, which later developed with over 40

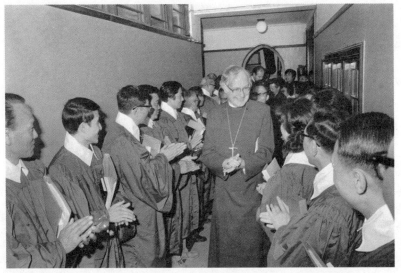

◎ Invited by Chinese People's Association for Friendship with Foreign Countries and China Christian Council, Archbishop of Canterbury Dr. Robert Runcie visited Shanghai, Hangzhou, Xi'an and Beijing from Dec.2nd to 17th, 1983. He was warmly welcomed by the Christians when he attended the Lord's Day services of the International Church in Shanghai.

affiliated churches.

Zou Liwen, a student in the Dengzhou Literature Association of the American Presbyterian Church in Shandong Province, worked on bible translation after his graduation. In 1885, with the assistance of over 40 of his schoolfellows, he established the Shandong Chou En Preaching Association. He declared that the new association was separated from the American Presbyterian Church and was independent, and had its own set of rules. The rules defined that any admitted member should donate money to sponsor its missionary and educational activities. All members paid their tributes actively, though they had only meager income. The famous young student priest Ding Limei and the translator Wang Xuanchen, who had independently translated the Bible, came from this association.

In the 20th century, the increasing mood of the Chinese people in their anti-imperialism patriotic struggles helped promote the development of the independent churches and pushed it from a kind of Chinese Christians' spontaneous act to a general movement. Many churches that were previously affiliated to the foreign mission systems declared independence. As a result, the independent churches emerged almost simultaneously in southern China, eastern China, Beijing, Tianjin and other places.

Shandong Province was the cradle of the Yi He Tuan Movement. Nearly 100 Shandong Christians were killed during that uprising. The Christians there were shocked by the local people's anti-foreign and anti-religious actions. In the late 19th century and early 20th century, there appeared many independent churches in Shandong, among which the independent association established by Liu Shoushan from the American Presbyterian Church was the most famous. Christians from other churches also originated some independent institutions. These independent churches operated affiliated facilities such as hospitals, schools, and old people's homes etc. All this showed that the development of independent churches had achieved some scale.

North China, with Beijing and Tianjin at its core, also became one of the focuses for the development of independent churches. In 1902, Zhong Zifeng, a Christian from the Presbyterian Church in Tianjin, united some Christians from the London Missionary Society, Congregational churches and other foreign missions to prepare for the establishment of an independent church. He was obstructed by some foreign priests and was forced to stop, but several years later his plan was raised again. In 1908, a Christian named Zhang Zhiting from the London Missionary Society appealed for the establishment of an

Evangelical Church of the Independence Association. In 1910, Xu Huichuan and Zhang Boling united their colleagues in different churches and established the Chinese Christian Church, which later admitted more than 600 believers. In some southern areas, like Guangdong, Hong Kong and Fujian Province, there also appeared many independent churches. In Guangdong Province, for example, many independent churches came into being after 1903, such as the Guangzhou Xing Hua Baptism Association, Guangzhou World-Relief Baptism Association, Guangzhou Presbyterian Association, etc. At that time, even those churches that had not yet gained a complete independence added 'China' or 'Chinese' ahead of their titles, just to show their determination to split with the foreign missions.

In Shanghai, worried about the repeated missionary incidents and the people's discontent, 13 Chinese Christians initiated the China Christian Association in 1903, appealing for their countrymen to unite and conduct missionary work independently. They also established a newspaper entitled The Christians to publicize the meaning of this independence. Their actions won the support of Christians from Hong Kong, Beijing, Tianjin, Ningbo and Tanyuan, who founded branch associations in these cities and did a lot of preparatory work in terms of winning over public opinion to promote the independence movement.

On this basis, Yu Guozhen, a Chinese Christian and priest, established the Association of Self-independence of Chinese Christian Churches in Shanghai in 1906. His aim of setting up this organization was to spread the gospel more effectively. He thought that the close relationship between the local churches and the foreign missions had led to people's misunderstanding that belief in religion meant giving up patriotism, which harmed the reputation of the churches. Only independence could eliminate this misunderstanding. He also advocated the integration or unification of different churches. In 1910, he united the churches that were willing to become independent in Zhejiang and Jiangsu provinces to form the General Association of Self-Independence of Chinese Christian Churches with Shanghai as its headquarters. After that, many independent churches were established one after another in Zhejiang, Fujian, Guangdong, Hubei and Hunan provinces. After the Xin Hai Revolution, this association made rapid development. In 1920, when the first national conference of the association was held, 130 representatives from more than 80 branches attended the meeting. The number of its branches was increasing on a year-to-year basis. By 1924, the association had altogether over 330 branches with about 20,000 believers.

In addition to the influence of the social environment, the reason why so many independent churches emerged in this period was also related to the fact that the human resources and economic conditions of the Christian churches had grown relatively mature. After more than half a century's development since Christianity had entered China, there had been lots of talented Chinese Christian leaders. In the early years of the 20th century, although the leadership of the Chinese churches was still controlled by the foreign missionaries and foreign missions, the number of Chinese clergymen had also started to grow. According to statistics in China for Christ, in 1907 when the first National

◎ In the morning of April 16, 1988, the famous U.S. Evangelicals leader Billy Graham visited the Temple of Heaven in Beijing with his wife.

Conference of the Chinese Christian Churches was held, all of the 1,000 attendees were foreign missionaries. However, when the second national conference was held in 1913, one third were Chinese. By 1919, when the Conference of China For Christ was held, Chinese representatives reached half of all participants. The Chinese Christian leaders had already shouldered part of the work in the churches, and in places where talented Chinese Christian leaders were relatively more concentrated, the leadership of the churches had been partly transferred to them. Some patriotic religious leaders began to recognize the historical mission they bore, and they did have the ability to lead the Chinese Christians to establish independent churches. The growth of talented Chinese Christians had worked as an intellectual base for the launch of the independence movement.

To the Chinese Christian churches, the foundation of independence was self-reliance. Without funds, independence could only be an empty word. At that time, Chinese industry had experienced some development and some patriotic industrialists and businessmen had become the mainstay for the self-reliance of the churches. For example, Liu Shoushan, initiator of the Qingdao Independence Church, was an industrialist engaged in real estate and construction, who invested a lot in the church.

Another priest named Wang Yuande, who had once worked in auto industry, also gave great financial support. Most of the independent churches were located in large or medium sized cities in the relatively developed coastal areas. On the one hand, the church leaders and Christians in these areas were more skillful in management, and on the other hand, the churches could have relatively more reliable sources of funds. The independent churches in southern China like Hong Kong, Guangdong and Fujian Provinces mainly relied on the support of overseas Chinese and had little problem in their financing. It proved that independent churches could hardly stick to their objectives when they were caught in financial difficulties, which could only lead to two results: either to go bankrupt or to resume their relations with the foreign missions. For instance, Shanghai Zha Bei Church fell into financial difficulties after it had lost some of its rich members' support. It could not even afford the printing expenses of its newspaper.

In this period, the independent churches were still in a situation of working individually and spontaneously. Because of the different social environments in which they operated, and their different religious backgrounds, they also had differing understandings about the concept of independence. Some churches cut all ties with the foreign missions and gained total independence. Most of them were once involved in clashes with the foreign missionaries who obstructed their moves towards independence. For example, when Liu Shoushan and his comrades were preparing for the establishment of an independent church in Jinan of Shandong Province, a foreign missionary from the American Presbyterian Church threatened to withdraw all the foreign missionaries. Fortunately, the local government supported their independence moves, so they did not fail. The independent churches in Zhejiang Province previously affiliated to the China Inland Mission, and the independent churches in Fujian Province previously affiliated to the Anglican Church, both broke their ties with their original foreign missions and joined the General Association of Self-Independence of Chinese Christian Churches.

Another type of independent church attached more importance to self-reliance and self-rule. Although they had renounced the foreign missions organizationally, they still maintained good relations with them. They declared independence more for religious reasons than political ones. They thought having a church run by Chinese was more conducive to the development of Christianity in China. The relationship between these churches and their original foreign missions was like that between students and teachers.

After the May 4th movement in 1919, the mood for the anti-imperialism struggle in China was running higher with each passing day. Many patriotic Chinese Christians also devoted themselves to this movement. Especially the May 30th Massacre in 1925 saw many Chinese Christian groups and believers gradually enhancing their patriotic awareness and getting to know the truth of imperialist aggression. They felt ashamed of the phenomenon that Christianity was called an alien religion and that Christians were called alien's slaves, and sought to split from imperialism and abolish the privileges grasped by the Christian Churches and prescribed in the unequal treaties. The churches in various places all announced their request of separating from foreign missions and establishing independent churches. When the national revolution reached a high tide in 1926, with the continuous military victories of the revolutionary forces, foreign missionaries ran away one after another and the independence movement of the churches developed further. In a short period of time, the trend of setting up independent churches swept over the entire country and over 600 were established during the revolution.

◎ A church on the seashore of Qingdao City, Shandong Province.

The greatest characteristic of the independent churches established in this period was that they were against imperialism as well as the protective articles laid down in the unequal treaties. Since the 1920s, the imperialist powers had intensified their aggression against China, with one bloody massacre after another, which all patriotic Christians and the people all over the country vehemently opposed. In 1925, a famous clergyman named Wang Yexin organized the Association of the Chinese Christians for Abolition of the Unequal Treaties, which was supported by patriotic Chinese Christians all over the country. Branches were established in many places like Nanchang, Guangzhou, Danyang, etc. A Christian conference held in Guangzhou requested the churches to sever their previous relations with the unequal treaties inflicted by the imperial powers and to help unite all circles in society to seek their abolition.

The independence movement of the Christian churches was in line with the development of history. However, it should be noted that, under the social circumstances at the times, the chief propellants of the movement were mainly the political enthusiasm and anti-imperialistic determination of various people, or the measures that sought the support of the people and to protect the churches. The churches themselves did not have enough organizational, financial and religious preparation. Places where the independence movement was active were all core areas of the national revolution, and the establishment of most of the independent churches was affected by the revolutionary tide. Therefore, when Chiang Kai-shek, leader of the KMT party, betrayed the revolution and the revolutionary tide began to subside, the independence movement began to fade away. The more than 600 independent churches that had appeared during the revolution were reduced to just 200 in 1935, with some suspending operations, some being disbanded and some returning to the arms of foreign missions.

2. *The Localization Movement of the Christian Churches to Remove Their Flavor of Western Culture*

Christianity was a religion to relieve ills of the world. The World Missionary Movement in the 19th century accompanying the colonial expansion of the European and American countries had enabled Christianity to forcibly enter the economically underdeveloped countries in Asia and Africa. However, Christianity, which was pervaded with Western culture, also met with cultural resistance by different ethnic groups in the course of its dissemination. In China, uninterrupted missionary cases, the Yi He Tuan Movement and the Non-Christian Movement had caused some foreign missionaries and Chinese Christian leaders to consider the profits and losses of the missionary undertaking in terms of culture. An indisputable fact was that, in many aspects, no matter in ideology, organization or etiquette, Christianity was incompatible with, and sometimes even clashed with, the Chinese indigenous culture. Thus, cultural estrangement hindered the development of Christianity in China. Thus, it was advocated not only by the Chinese Christian leaders to localize Christianity by neutralizing its Western coloring, but also by some foreign missionaries in the early times who had tried to explain Christianity with traditional Confucian ideology, but failed because the culture differences were too hard to overcome.

The World Missionary Convention held in Edinburgh in 1900 was a turning point in that it concluded 'the time had past that the different churches could operate and complete their missionary work independently', and the functions of churches in different dioceses throughout the world should be highlighted to promote the localization movement. In 1913, John Mott, one of the chief leaders of the Protestant International Organization, came to China to research the missionary plan. After visiting six cities like Guangzhou, Shanghai, Jinan, Beijing, etc, he held the National Conference of the Chinese Christian Churches in Shanghai, which was attended by 120 church leaders. According to the situation faced by the churches, the conference proposed that it should urge the Chinese Christians to take on the responsibility of preaching.

Mott came to Shanghai again in May 1922 to hold another national conference, this time attended by 1,200 representatives from more than 70 foreign missions, among whom half were Chinese clergy. The main theme was 'the Chinese Churches'. It focused on specific Chinese problems such as preaching, education, publication, charity and women, etc, and put forward the proposition of 'Localized Churches', believing that the prosperity of Chinese churches rested on 'Integration and Localization'. The conference approved the proposal to establish a National Christian Council of China, and appointed two Chinese Christians Yu Rizhang and Cheng Jingyi as president and secretary general respectively. The council aimed at even more vigorous promotion of the localization movement. Although Yu Rizhang and Cheng Jingyi were both Chinese, the council still could not escape from the control of the foreign missions and missionaries, and was just a union of different foreign missions in China, with its chief directors of all committees being foreign missionaries, while all the meetings were staged in English, and all reports, discussions and minutes were also in English. So, it was obvious that the localization movement under the control of the foreign missionaries could only be a cosmetic move.

In the 1920s, facing various kinds of anti-religion ideology in society, localization that should have been pushed ahead solely by the Chinese themselves had become an imperative for Chinese

Christianity. Since the 1920s, lots of Chinese Christian intellectuals such as Cheng Jingyi, Zhao Zichen, Wu Leichuan, etc, had begun to explore means of achieving localization. All of them had extensive knowledge about traditional Chinese culture and held a rational view towards their belief in Christianity. They were keen on finding a way out from Christianity to save the country and were worried about the foreign coloring of the Chinese Christian churches. They naturally became the active driving force of the localization movement.

Cheng Jingyi, secretary general of the National Christian Council of China, made some penetrating comments on the localization issue: 'Localization of churches as advocated by the council requires Chinese Christians to take on the responsibility for rejuvenating the innate essence of oriental civilization and to remove the bad reputation as a foreign religion burdened by Christianity.' There were two meanings to his words: first, Chinese Christians should be responsible to themselves, namely, the Chinese churches should practice independence with Chinese Christians playing the key role; second, Chinese Christians should rejuvenate the inherent oriental civilization and absorb its essence to neutralize the foreign flavor of Christianity and get it across to the Chinese people.

◎ The Chinese Churches attach great importance to academic research. This was a symposium held in Dalian in July 1993.

Among all the leaders of the Chinese Christian Churches, Zhao Zichen talked relatively more about localization than others. He had a good command of both Chinese and English, and was good at presenting Christian theology in the form of Chinese traditional culture. Many of his works won praise from the people, such as Christian Philosophy in the form of fiction and dialogue, and The Legend of Jesus Christ that combined history, biography and literature. In the course of the localization of the Christian Churches, he considered that Chinese Christianity should become a part of Chinese culture. The prospect he depicted for the localized Churches was like this: 'they should integrate all truths

© A church in Dong Mountain in Guangzhou.

generated by Christianity and the ancient Chinese culture and make Chinese Christians' religious lives and experiences accord with the national situation. Developing in this form for some time, the localized Churches are supposed to be managed by the Chinese themselves economically, organizationally and theologically. Without this being realized, the localization of the Christian churches in China will be incomplete.'

From the 1920s, discussions about the localization of the Christian churches in China had been very heated. Many publications published articles, not only pointing out the necessity and imperativeness of the localization, but also putting forward some concrete plans as to its theoretical guidance.

There were three directions for the localization movement initiated by the Chinese Christian Churches, namely: independence, integration and localization. Many churches made helpful explorations and experiments on the above-mentioned three directions to promote the movement.

INDEPENDENCE

In the years of pressing ahead with the localization of Churches, several major churches previously controlled by foreign missions all added 'China' ahead of their names. However, their leadership still rested in the hands of foreign missionaries, and the churches still relied on financial support from the foreign missions. The leaders of the Chinese Churches also had contradictory feelings about these facts. On the one hand, they wanted independence from the foreign missions, while at the same time, being part of the movement to spread Christianity throughout the world, they did not want to be totally separated from the foreign missions. What they thought was the best model was that Chinese Christians should take over the local work while still cooperating with the Western missionaries, who would retain a position in the churches. However, this could only be an ideal and was very hard to realize. Actually, most of the Churches in the 1920s did not have a great number of members or enough funds, and could barely win financial independence, while the Western missionaries could offer the churches financial support through the foreign missions. Economic support simply meant control in management. Therefore, the independence movement could not survive despite having undergone vigorous development. That was why Zhao Zichen wrote in Some of My Opinions on Creating Chinese Christian Churches that, 'If the Churches were run by Chinese Christians, they would fall short in funds and talent'. He pointed out in 1927 that one of the major reasons for the unsatisfactory results of the localization movement was 'no organization of localized churches had been created.'

INTEGRATION

The Christian doctrine of 'Justification by Faith' provided large room for the free development of the churches. There were so many factions in the Christian world with each running separately and individually. After China's door was opened, many religious groups came to preach on their own. According to statistics in the History of the Chinese Christian Churches, the total number of foreign missions and missionary groups coming to China exceeded 130. To a Chinese Christian, the Western sectarian tradition was meaningless and had nothing to do with his religious life. What is more, it had hindered the union of the Christian Churches and affected their work, which the Chinese Christians felt greatly

◎ He Nan Church in Guangzhou, which has some ethnic architectural features

discontented about. Zhao Zichen pointed out that narrow-minded sectarianism could only impair and endanger the churches in China. As a matter of fact, he would not have opposed sectarianism in the Christian world if it had simply been an expression of diversified faiths. However, different factions disputed with each other on theological issues to the extent that nobody cared about the overall task. It was exactly this result that he felt uncomfortable with.

In the localization movement, the union of different churches became the unanimous request of Chinese Christians. Some had the churches in the same faction united to form a large group. For instance, the different Anglican churches united as the China Anglican Churches, as did the General Presbyterian Churches. Some proposed that the different Christian factions in one city to merge into a big organization, for instance, to form a China Christian Churches in Guangdong and Southern Fujian, etc. Some proposed that all Churches should be unified and governed by Chinese. Some suggested establishing an organization to discuss on different issues, regardless of the union of the Churches in formality. And some proposed to merge the churches according to the specific trade they fell in, like China Christian Churches of Education, etc. Shanghai even established the Chinese Home Missionary Society specially for preaching in the inland areas.

Among all the localized Churches, the biggest was Church of Christ in China. After years of preparations, the first National Assembly of Church of Christ in China was held in Shanghai in October 1927. Among the 88 attendees, 66 were Chinese Christian leaders who represented 12 dioceses, 51 parishes and more than 120,000 Christians or 1/3rd of all the Chinese Christians. Most of the representatives were from Presbyterian churches. The assembly elected Chen Jingyi president of the organization, making it clear that all member churches must abandon their original sectarian thoughts and push the localization movement forward on the principle of 'anti-sectarianism and integration', so as to reach the objective of all Chinese churches being unified into one. The Church of Christ in China was formed as a result. It only sought to conform to the specific Chinese situation and to meet Chinese needs, without being separated by different factions or countries.

LOCALIZATION

How should Christianity be integrated with Chinese culture and appreciated by the Chinese people was by no means an easy task. By culture, it included not only its outside formality but more importantly its internal spirit. By comparison, changes or integrations in terms of formality were much easier. In some places, the churches were built in the traditional Chinese way and chants were composed with a Chinese melody. In 1931, Zhao Zichen wrote lyrics for the chants and published a brochure containing them. A Christian organization set up in Shanghai in 1927 composed over 50 new Chinese poems in order to create a model for the localization of churches. Christians in this organization utilized some traditional Chinese ethnic musical instruments to accompany the poems. They also changed the layout of the church, moving the platform aside and setting up a chancel in the middle of the church with a bronze stove in front of it. When there was to be preaching, the smoke of the incense burned in the bronze stove would curl upward, and the worshippers would pray on bended knees in front of the chancel. The priest was dressed in the traditional Chinese way. Actually, there were quite a lot of warmhearted Christians in different places who were experimenting on the integration of Christianity with Chinese culture.

It was also a sensitive issue concerning how to treat the

◎ A church of Va nationality in Taojin Village, Lancang County, Yunnan Province

Chinese traditional ancestor worship rituals. If the rituals had been banned in the light of some missionaries' criticisms that they were a kind of idolatry, Christianity would have been separated from Chinese culture and most of the Chinese people. Chen Jingyi proposed a compromise that, in a defined period of time, all the Chinese Christians go to the cemetery to hold worship ceremonies together. He thought this was not in conflict with the doctrines of Christianity, but suited the Chinese people's logic, and was a means of localization of Christianity. Wang Yexin also thought some elements of the Chinese culture, like the Chinese ethics, spirit of hardworking and behavior of faith, could complement Western culture.

In 1924, the Standing Committee for Localized Churches established by the National Christian Council of China raised some subjects for research: 1) a variety of immortal values in Chinese culture, like the perception of family life, filial piety, mentality of peace and modesty, etc; 2) the movements of all kinds of Chinese religious groups in modern times; 3) the organization, theory and leadership of the Non-Religion Movement; 4) the current situation of the independent Churches in China; 5) the relationship between foreign missions and the Chinese churches; 6) all kinds of rituals in the Chinese churches.

It was a huge and thorough research plan aimed at having a deep understanding of Chinese culture and religion, the criticisms at the Non-Religion Movement and Christianity itself, so as to find a more appropriate way for the Chinese people to represent their faith on Christianity. Of course, it was a rather tough task that needed continuous exploration and practice. The road of localization would be very long for the Chinese churches.

Chapter 4
Three-Self Patriotic Movement of the Chinese Churches

1. Christianity Facing the Choice of New China

In 1949, with the continuous victories of the People's Liberation Army, the founding of a new China was becoming an overwhelming trend. Quite a lot of Christians were considering the question: what should Chinese churches do in the future? For a long time, the foreign missionaries in China, especially American missionaries, had taken it as one of their major tasks to oppose communism, and had missed no opportunity to make anti-communist speeches, in an attempt to train Chinese churches into forces opposing the Communist Party of China (CPC).

Influenced by the foreign missionaries, the Christian churches, schools and publications were full of pro-American and anti-communist ideology and comments, which deeply affected many Christians. After the victory of the War of Resistance against Japanese Aggression, Chiang Kai-shek broke his own words and provoked civil war. Considering American interests and for some ideological reasons, American missionaries took the churches as a tool to carry out their anti-communist propaganda and incited the sentiments of anti-communism and anti-Sovietism among Chinese Christians. In December 1942, when the 13th annual meeting of the National Christian Council of China was held, some missionaries were specially invited to make such anti-communist speeches as 'Christianity and Communism', 'the Churches and the New Epoch', etc. They proposed to fight against the dissemination of the communist ideology with the 'Pushing Ahead Movement'. John Leighton Stuart, the U.S. ambassador to China at that time, repeatedly instructed the missionaries to attach great importance to the construction of churches in rural China and to compete with CPC in winning the loyalty of the peasantry. The time from 1947 to 1949 was the period that the Chinese communist revolution achieved a series of decisive victories, but the anti-communist trend in the churches became

◎ In 1998, the choir of Jinling Concord Theological College gained the second prize in the Nanjing Jinling Chorus Festival.

more rampant. The book Atomic Bomb and the End of the World published by the Seventh Day Adventists described the communist parties' capture of regimes as the end of the world. And 110,000 copies of its first edition were printed which exercised a rather large influence. With the liberation of various places in north China, the foreign missionaries and some Chinese clergy ran to the south one after another and made speeches to the churches there. They said they had witnessed the CPC killing people and committing all kinds of crimes, and spread rumors that the CPC persecuted religious people in an attempt to provoke Christian anti-communist sentiments. The college magazine of

◎ The new church of Hu Dong Church built up in 1997 in Shanghai can accommodate a gathering of 3,000 Christians.

Nanjing Jinling Concord Theological College carried a story that a priest in Shandong Province was nailed dead on the Cross. However, soon after the whole country was liberated, this priest whose name was mentioned in the magazine came to Nanjing himself, which naturally scotched that rumor. Some clergymen even used the prophesies of Bible to attack the CPC by innuendo, saying that the half-iron, half-clay feet of the giant described in the book of Daniel was the union of workers and farmers, which would be broken down in the future; and that the locust and the red horse in the book of Revelations were bombers and the communist party, and one third of the people on the earth would be killed by them. These inflammatory remarks stirred up one upsurge after another in the Chinese churches. Before the KMT regime fled to Taiwan and the foreign missionaries ran away from the Chinese mainland, the latter planned a series of emergency measures. These included: launching a 'Saving the Soul Movement'; training Chinese clergymen to replace the foreign missionaries and seeking opportunities to carry out disruptive activities under complicated circumstances; to integrate the churches into families to disseminate disruptive activities, etc. They attempted to deprave Christian churches to tools of the American and KMT reactionary forces. Therefore, after the founding of the People's Republic of China, many Christians did not trust the communist regime and felt there was no future under it.

Meanwhile, there were still some Christians actively welcoming the establishment of the new China and Wu Yaozong was one of them. He had participated in the struggle against the Japanese invaders, and through his contacts with the communists he had gradually come to know and understand the CPC's ideas. After the victory against Japan, he took part in the democratic movement to protest against autocracy and civil war, but was assaulted by KMT special agents. Wu thought that the mission of Christianity was to 'work as a driving force in the progressive revolutionary course', but, at a time when Chinese society was undergoing grave changes, those Christian churches were still adhering to the old practices and had become defenders of the old social system. He was deeply worried about this phenomenon and hoped the churches could catch up with the development of the times. On Easter day in 1948, he wrote an article entitled Christianity's Tragedy of the Times, in which he pointed out that the traditions of Chinese Christianity were mainly derived from the U.S., the Christian leaders were mainly trained in the U.S., many important organizations and undertakings were sponsored by American churches, and their faith and ideology were almost a reprint of American Christianity. Although China was facing an unprecedented transformation in its history, many Chinese Christians followed the 'new Crusade line' and were virtually transformed into a tool of the imperialists and their cultural aggression. He warned at the end of the article that, 'The trend of the times will go ahead. If our religion is superstitious, backward, and against the benefits of the people, what we have done will surely be cruelly exposed and punished by history. Until that time, if we still thought we were compelled to do so by our faith and were entrusted by Jesus Christ, that would be even more deplorable'. Before the founding of the new China, Wu Yaozong had already penetratingly perceived the problems in Chinese Christianity. He was one of the few patriotic 'prophets' in the Chinese Christian churches at that time.

From Sept. 21 to Sept. 30, 1949, just before the People's Republic of China was founded, the Chinese People's Political Consultative Conference (CPPCC) was held in Beijing. Altogether eight religious deputies were invited to the meeting, among whom five were from Christian circles, two from Buddhism and one from Islam. The five Christian deputies were Wu Yaozong, Deng Yuzhi, Zhao Zichen, Liu Liangmo and Zhang

◎ The eight religious committee members of the first CPPCC. Five of them were Christians: Wu Yaozong (the third on the front left), Deng Yuzhi (the first on the front left), Zhao Zichen (the fourth on the front left), Zhang Xueyan (the second on the behind left), and Liu Liangmo (the first on the behind left).

Xueyan. In the Joint Guidelines approved by the CPPCC session, it was clearly defined that all Chinese people enjoyed the freedom of religious belief. In his speech, Wu Yaozong stated: 'Religion has occupied its due position in the plan of the construction of new China. The principle of freedom of religious belief has been clarified in the Joint Guidelines. We cherish this freedom, and will never let the freedom down or abuse it. We will also try our utmost to stamp out the depraved and vicious traditions in Chinese Christianity and to uproot its ties with the feudalists and imperialists of the past. We are ready to follow all the democrats and democratic parties to fight for this joint objective.'

As to the status and conditions of Christianity in the new China, there were also debates aroused by the Christians. On Jun. 17, 1949, Dagong Bao (one of the most popular newspapers in Shanghai) carried a letter from five Christians in an article entitled The Awakening of the Christians in its social service column, mainly dealing with their opposition to the imperialists making use of Christianity. This letter aroused strong feedback among Christians and many people wrote articles to express their

◎ In September 1949, Wu Yaozong made a speech in the CPPCC sessions.

views. At the same time, the Christian magazine Wind of the Heaven also published articles written by quite a number of Christians, discussing the role Christianity should play in the new epoch. Many expressed their dissatisfaction about Christianity's lagging behind the times. The facts demonstrated that a lot of Christians had awakened and were ready to march into the new epoch and a bright future.

2. The Emergence of Three-Self Declaration

The founding of the People's Republic of China in 1949 symbolized that the Chinese people had stood up and become the master of their own affairs. Patriotic Chinese Christians welcomed this great event along with the entire people of the country. The Joint Guidelines approved by the first CPPCC session made clear the issue of freedom of religious belief. However, as a 'foreign religion', Christianity still posed some contradictions for the Chinese people. In the large-scale revolutionary movements, the Christian Churches in many places inevitably suffered some destruction, and cases of churches being damaged or occupied during wartime occurred repeatedly.

In the spring of 1950, in order to publicize the essence of the CPPCC session and to know more about the situation of the churches in different places, Wu Yaozong and other patriotic Christians organized a team and visited different parts of the country. After the tour, he came to Beijing and made a report to Premier Zhou Enlai on the difficulties the churches were facing.

To find ways to overcome these difficulties, Premier Zhou convened three meetings with the Christian representatives respectively on May 2nd, May 6th and May 13th, 1950. Altogether 18 representatives were invited. Premier Zhou appreciated the principles of self-rule, self-reliance and self-development (or three-self principle) mentioned by Wu Yaozong, reaffirmed the CPC's policy on the freedom of religious belief, and acknowledged that the existence of religions was long term.

◎ On 23rd Sep. 1950, the People's Daily carried the full text of the Three-self Announcement as well as the name list of the first batch of 1,527 supporters of the announcement.

一九五一年四月廣州中華基督教會仁濟堂教友 315 人在「革新宣言」上簽名

◎ Over 420,000 Christian believers in Guangzhou signed their names on the Three-self Announcement, almost accounting to 2/3 of the total Christians in the country.

He pointed out that materialists and ideologists could co-operate politically, and correspondingly they could co-exist in the country and should respect each other.

Enlightened by Premier Zhou, the Christian leaders realized that the difficulties Christianity faced were due to its notorious history being connected to Western colonialism. Only by seeking approaches to obtain the people's trust, not by 'orders' from the government could Christianity win the Chinese people's understanding and acknowledgement. That was to say, Christianity must 'actively sweep away the imperialist powers and influences within itself'. After the Christian team returned to

Shanghai, 40 Chinese Christian leaders headed by Wu Yaozong eventually drafted an announcement after much discussion, meditation and modification. The title of the announcement was Approaches to the Work of the Chinese Christian Churches during the Construction of the New China, abbreviated to the Three-Self Announcement. As the initiators of the announcement, the 40 Chinese Christian leaders sent an open letter to all Christian Churches and organizations in China, appealing to all Chinese Christians to clearly understand the historical fact that Christianity had been exploited by imperialism and to work out a detailed plan to realize self-rule, self-reliance and self-development as soon as possible. The Three-Self Announcement quickly gained support all over the country, with the first batch of 1,527 Christians signing their names to it. The announcement was also backed by social opinion. On September 23rd 1950, the People's Daily published the Three-Self Announcement, as well as the letter of the 40 initiators. They also published an editorial entitled The Patriotic Movement of the Christians, pointing out: 'This is a patriotic movement that the Chinese Christians are bound to launch so as to get rid of the imperialist influence and furthermore push ahead on the right religious track.' It also stated that it was a 'thriving revolution of reform, ... and the success of the revolution will grant Chinese Christianity a new life and change the Chinese people's perception of Christianity, because it has made a clear division of its religious activities from the aggressive moves of the imperial forces in China.' The Three-Self Announcement received a warm welcome from all Chinese Christians, including those in many remote areas. By September 25th, another batch of more than 1,500 people had become signatories. A massive three-self movement had been waged in the churches. By September 1953, the total number of signatories had reached 400,000.

3. A New Stage of Three-Self Patriotic Movement

With the outbreak of the Korean War in June 1950, Sino-U.S. relations quickly worsened. On 16th December 1950, the U.S. government announced it was taking control of all Chinese and North Korean possessions in all areas under its jurisdiction, and prohibited any ships registered in the U.S. from heading for Chinese ports. However, this blockade meant that the Christian churches, schools, hospitals and charity organizations that relied heavily on American subsidies suffered greatly. Because of the cut of subsidies and the urgent situation, foreign missionaries ran away one after another and consequently the Chinese churches were confronted with great difficulties. The Chinese government promptly provided care and help, exempting churches from taxes on the direct use of houses and taking over their educational and medicine institutions, which greatly alleviated their economic burden. Christians expressed their support for the decision made by the government. On Jan. 5th, 1951, 26 Christian leaders of the national and local Christian organizations in Shanghai published a declaration to show their support of the decision, announcing that 'directed by the spirit of patriotism and self-respect, we could not only get rid of our old economic relationship with the U.S. as its tool of cultural aggression, but also rely on ourselves to build up a more healthy Christian cause that could better serve society'.

The actions by the U.S. government to threaten the Chinese churches by cutting off the funds backfired and aroused more vigorous opposition in Christian circles and the patriotic passion of Chinese Christians. They enthusiastically signed the Three-Self Announcement, and many Christian groups immediately announced that, from 1951 on, they would no longer accept any subsidies in any form from the U.S. and other countries. All Christian churches, groups as well as the local churches registered with the government. According to the original plan, the goal of self-rule, self-reliance and self-development of the Chinese churches would have been achieved gradually in five years, but under the interference of the U.S. government, the plan had to be carried out ahead of time. In April 1951, the Joint Proclamation of all the Chinese Christian Churches adopted in a national conference called on all the Christians to cut all their ties with foreign churches; realize the three-self principle; wholeheartedly join the anti- U.S. campaign; support the joint guideline, land reform and policies on oppressing counter-revolutionists; observe all laws and regulations made by the government; strengthen patriotic education and launch an extensive study movement. This proclamation made a step further compared with the Three-Self Announcement and fully demonstrated Chinese Christians' confidence in becoming independent and enjoying self-rule.

This conference also established 'The Committee of the Chinese Christian Churches for the Anti-U.S. Pro-Korean War and the Three-Self Renovation Movement (Preparative Committee)', and approved the name list of the committee. Wu Yaozong was appointed chairman. This committee became a new national leadership for Chinese Christianity to push ahead the anti-imperialist and patriotic movement under the principle of the three-self renovation.

4. Establishment of National Committee of Three-self Patriotic Movement of the Protestant Church in China

On the consolidated basis of the four-year three-self renovation movement, in order to set up the policy and tasks for the work in the future and deepen the movement, The Committee of the Chinese Christian Churches for the Anti-U.S. Pro-Korean War and the Three-Self Renovation Movement held a national meeting from July 22nd to Aug. 6th, 1954. Altogether 232 representatives from all over the country attended from 62 Christian Churches and groups.

During the meeting, Wu Yaozong made a work report about the four-year three-self renovation movement. He summed up the achievements in four aspects: 1) the Chinese Christian Churches and groups had basically emerged from imperial control and had gradually developed into religious groups ruled by the Chinese Christians themselves; 2) the movement to stamp out imperialist influence inside Christianity had been started; 3) all

◎ In April 1953, Wu Yaozong (the third on the front left), Xie Yongqin (the fourth on the front left) and Han Wenzao (the first on the front left), etc visited the churches in Zhejiang and Fujian provinces to promote the three-self movement. They were welcomed by a priest named Shu Shunyuan (the second on the front left) at a church in Jin County.

Christians in the country had improved their understanding of anti-imperialism and patriotism, and had taken part in all kinds of patriotic movements as well as movements aimed at protecting world peace; 4) the churches of the new China had taken a turn for the better on the basis of patriotism and loyalty to Christianity.

In his speech, Wu also put forward the policies and tasks in the future in seven aspects: 1) to appeal to all the Christians to support the constitutional law of the People's Republic of China and to work hard for the construction of a socialist society; 2) to appeal to all the Christians to protest against the imperial aggression and struggle for the long term world peace; 3) to continue patriotic education among all Christian clergy and believers so as to totally stamp out the influence of imperialism; 4) to earnestly practice the spirit of self-rule and promote unity inside Christian churches; 5) to research the problem of self-reliance and assist the churches to overcome this problem; 6) to research the work of self-development and spread pure evangelism under the principle of mutual respect; 7) to stick to the spirit of patriotism and loyalty to Christianity, observe the law and purify the churches.

After a general discussion, the conference adopted A Letter to All Chinese Christians by the National Conference of Chinese Christianity, modifying 'renovation' to 'patriotic' so as to eliminate unnecessary worries and misunderstandings. The new national institution was thus renamed the 'National Committee of Three-Self Patriotic Movement of the Protestant Church in China'.

The conference adopted the guidelines for the committee, elected 139 committee members and obtained wide representation. Wu Yaozong was elected chairman of the committee. Chen Jianzhen, Wu Yifang, Chen Conggui, Jiang Changchuan, Cui Jianxiang, Ding Yuzhang were elected vice chairmen. To show sincere unity, the committee also reserved 11 positions for possible additional members in future.

The conference also approved four resolutions: 1) With the common objective of anti-imperialism, patriotism and loyalty to Christianity, the unity of all Christians in all churches should be achieved and the three-self movement should be carried out continuously; in terms of the differences in beliefs, systems and reverence rituals among different Churches, the principle of mutual respect should be adopted. 2) All the Chinese Christians must support the draft edition of the constitutional law of the People's Republic of China, and work hard together with all the Chinese people to build the socialist society; they should also cherish the rights of freedom of religious belief prescribed in the draft constitution, promise not to abuse this right to carry out activities against the interests of the people, advocate patriotism and observation of the law and perform their due obligations as a citizen. 3) The committee should appeal to all the Christians in China to actively take part in the movement to protect world peace and strongly oppose the U.S. imperialist occupation of the Chinese territory of Taiwan. 4) The committee should encourage all Christians to continue their patriotic studies and to stamp out the remaining influence of imperialism, discern right from wrong as well as virtue from evil, and purify the churches.

After four years of hard work in the three-self patriotic movement, the new national Christian institution was established and independence achieved. The Chinese Christian churches achieved a fundamental change both in organization and in ideology and Christianity had become a religious cause operated by the Chinese Christians themselves. Later, the local committees for the three-self patriotic movement were established in different provinces, municipalities and autonomous regions successively.

5. *Three Witnesses and Ten Tasks*

From 15th May to 23rd May 1956, the National Committee of Three-Self Patriotic Movement of the Protestant Church in China held the second conference in Beijing. Altogether 249 representatives attended the conference. Wu Yaozong made a report entitled A Report on the Three-Self Patriotic Movement of the Protestant Church in China. The report summarized the development of the movement started in 1954, and raised the principles and tasks for the work in the future, which could be described as 'three witnesses' and 'ten tasks'. 'Three witnesses' pointed out the direction of development and required Chinese Christians to witness to God's deeds and orders in the specific times in which they lived. The details were: to witness to the realization of self-rule, self-reliance and self-development of the Chinese churches; to witness the participation of socialist construction; to witness the work to protect world peace. The 'Ten Tasks' were the detailed work plans, including: 1) to further consolidate and expand church unity; 2) each church should straighten out its own organization, personnel and economy so as to strengthen the leadership, set up a proper system and improve its work; 3) to establish a Committee of the Chinese churches for Promotion of Self-Reliance, which should fully consider the necessity of church self-reliance, collect funds through various channels, and try to resolve the self-reliance problem of the churches by the end of 1957; 4) hold meetings to research self-development, and set up a standing institution responsible for the work in this regard; 5) to vigorously encourage development in the Christian publication sector, and assist the Christian publishing houses in improving their work and quality; 6) to make full use of the books and materials in the Christian churches and groups to conduct research on theology, history of the churches and their work; 7) to make full use of the possible potentials and draw out a plan to train more talented qualified people for the Chinese churches; 8) to appeal to all Chinese Christians to actively take part in the construction of the socialist motherland together with the people in other circles; 9) to promote international friendship and co-operation and support various efforts of the Christians in different countries to achieve world peace; 10) greatly enhance the Christians' study of socialism and promote their enthusiasm in constructing socialism.

The 'three witnesses' and 'ten tasks' upheld the clear direction of development and the detailed contents of work for the three-self patriotic movement of the Chinese churches, and was the base for the healthy development of the movement. Unfortunately, from the late 1950s to the 1960s, due to the disturbances of the leftist ideology, Chinese socialist construction became derailed, and the tasks of the three-self patriotic movement did not proceed smoothly. And the 10-year 'Cultural Revolution' from 1966 to 1976 brought disaster to the entire people and greatly disrupting the work environment and the social order. Religions also suffered a lot. The Christian churches had to be closed, the religious activities of Christians were banned, and the three-self patriotic movement had to stop work.

CHAPTER 5
CHINESE CHURCHES DURING THE PERIOD OF REFORM AND OPENING UP TO THE OUTSIDE WORLD

1. The Restoration and Development of the Chinese Churches

In 1978, China started to adopt the policy of reform and opening up to the outside world. The Chinese Christian churches began to rejuvenate in an all-round manner. In May 1980, the National Committee of the Three-Self Patriotic Movement of the Protestant Church in China convened its third general conference. The conference was held 20 years after the second conference was held in 1960 and thus had profound meaning. The conference adopted the amendment of the committee's guidelines and set up a new leadership. To better promote the routine affairs of the

107

churches, the conference also established the China Christian Council. The difference between the 'National Committee of Three-Self Patriotic Movement of the Protestant Church in China' and 'China Christian Council' were as follows: the former was a patriotic organization, and its main task was to unite all Chinese Christians in the spirit of patriotism and to operate the churches according to the principle of self-rule, self-reliance and self-development. The latter was an organization to handle the everyday businesses of the churches and to promote the development of theological education, publication, etc. The conference elected Bishop Ding Guangxun chairman of the National Committee of Three-Self Patriotic Movement of the Protestant Church in China and president of China Christian Council. After the conference, the local branches of the two organizations were set up at provincial, municipal and township level successively.

From the late 1970s to the mid 1980s, the primary task of the Chinese churches was to support the government in its work to implement State policy on religion that had been disrupted during the Cultural Revolution as soon as possible, and to reopen the places and churches for religious activities. With the efforts of the two organizations at both national and local levels, the

◎ During the sixth national conference of the Christian Churches (Dec. 1996- Jan. 1997), the directors in chief of the two organizations presented wreaths to Mr. and Mrs. Wu Yaozong.

implementation of the policy made great progress. On 8th April 1979, the Bai Nian Church in Ningbo of Zhejiang Province took the lead in restoring the preaching ceremony; on 26th August of the same year, Xin Jie Church in Xiamen of Fujian Province reopened; and on 2nd September, Mu'en Church, which is located in central Shanghai, reopened with a preaching ceremony, which many Christians hailed as great news. Later on, churches in different places reopened one after another and an upsurge of restoring churches and building new ones began. Since the rapid increase in the number of Christians as well as the lack of

◎ A fixed gathering place was established in Lu County of Sichuan Province.

churches and Christian estates in many places, the two organizations actively communicated with the local governments, and built and expanded many churches and gathering venues to meet the Christians' religious needs. In some areas inhabited by ethnic minorities, churches with special ethnic features were built. According to statistics from the two organizations, there were more than 4,000 churches in the country in 1986, and more than 7,000 in 1991. By 1996, there were 12,000 churches and more than 25,000 gathering places. At present, there are nearly 50,000 churches and family gathering places in the country, 70% of them in rural areas. These churches have basically met the Christians' needs to participate in religious activities.

In addition to normal religious services, churches and gathering places hold different kinds of activities to satisfy the demands of the Christians, for example, Bible reading gatherings, prayer gatherings, youth gatherings, choir, summer and winter gatherings; when Christmas Day, Good Friday or Easter Sunday come round, all kinds of ceremonies are held; besides, marriage services, funeral services, commemoration and retrospection services, respecting the elderly services and different kinds of thanksgiving services all proceed as normal. Chinese Christians still maintain the good tradition of going to church together without discrimination between different factions, which has been followed since 1958. Under the principle of caring for all different religious factions and showing mutual respect among different religious beliefs, the Chinese government also gives special

◎ Christians of some ethnic minorities in Yunnan Province were praying.

consideration to those who have specific demands in terms of belief or rituals. For instance, Sabbath gatherings are held in some places; and both infusion and immersion, the two forms of baptism, are practiced freely. Some churches provided dialect preaching and blind Christians' gatherings to serve those who need special care; for those Christians who were old, weak or live far from the church, services like visiting preaching, communion etc are offered so as to let them feel the care of the churches like everyone else.

In the more and more relaxed social environment, freedom of religious belief is respected and protected. The number of Christians has risen greatly. In the nearly 150 years between 1807 and 1949 when foreign missionaries tried hard to spread Christianity, there were only 700,000 believers. After 1949, for various reasons, the number of Christians fell a little. However, since 1979, Chinese Christianity has made rapid development. According

◎ Wang Jinlian, a Christian in Ruian County of Zhejiang Province, was a national model worker in agriculture.

◎ In 1987, Wang Juzhen was awarded the National Invention Prize. She was the only winner of the first prize that year. She was introducing her invention to the then state councilor Song Jian.

to statistics, there were three million Christians in China in 1979, while the number jumped to 16 million in 2002. And among the five biggest religions in China, Christianity was one that developed the fastest. In geographical terms, provinces like Henan, Anhui, Jiangsu and Zhejiang developed relatively faster than elsewhere.

In another development, the admission of large number of new members has brought some changes to the composition of Christianity in China. In the past, the majority of Chinese Christians had always been working people and intellectuals, with 70% of Christians living in rural areas. They were characterized by four 'many's, namely, many elderly people, many women, many illiterates and many sick people. In the 1990s, the ratio of middle-aged people, youths and intellectuals rose slightly. To enhance the newly admitted Christians' quality in their faith, Christian churches at various levels spared no efforts in helping them shake off the influence of superstition, resist unlawful activities and set up the right faith. The churches also encouraged Christians to serve other people's needs on different occasions, for example, among families, neighborhoods and in the community and workplace, and to be a witness to God's virtues. Many Christians had no knowledge about Christianity at the very beginning, but have developed a relatively purified faith and improved a lot in their consciousness of God. After they embraced Christianity, many Christians felt that their lives became more meaningful with set goals and their hearts and minds became peaceful and cheerful. They observe the Ten Commandments and are compassionate. Some of them have improved their family lives as well as their relations with their neighbors; some have regretted past wrongdoings and sworn to mend their ways; in many places, there have appeared some Christians who pursue truth, devote themselves to God and are always ready to give. They have greatly improved the image of Christianity. At present, a lot of excellent Christians have played an active role in the material and spiritual construction of the socialist country. For instance, Wang Juzhen, a female Christian in Shanghai Mu En Church, invented 'tungsten cerium electrode' after years of researches and trials and won many national and international prizes. She was elected a deputy of the People's Congress of Shanghai Municipality and a member of the CPPCC. Many excellent Christians like Wang Juzhen emerge every year, and they are granted various prizes. They include college professors, scientists, medical workers, teachers, businessmen, and more often ordinary workers and farmers. All of them have brought glory to their faith and have won the people's trust through their loyalty to the country and Christianity.

2. The Establishment and Perfection of Organizations of Churches in Line with the Three-self Principle

The establishment and perfection of National Committee of Three-Self Patriotic Movement of the Protestant Church in China and its institution for routine affairs provided a solid foundation for the smooth running of their work. More than 1700 national or local branches of the 'China Christian Council' and 'Committee of Three-Self Patriotic Movement' have been established. From 1980 to 2002, the Chinese Christian Churches held four national conferences, namely the fourth National Conference on Christianity in 1986, the fifth in 1991, the sixth 1996 and the seventh in 2002. At the seventh conference, Ji Jianhong was elected chairman of the National Committee of the Three-Self Patriotic Movement of the Protestant Church in China, and Cao Shengjie was elected president of the China Christian Council.

To promote all kinds of church work, the 'National Committee of Three-Self Patriotic Movement of the Protestant

◎ In October 1980, the third national conference of the Christian Churches was held in Nanjing.

Church in China' and the 'China Christian Council' (referred to as two organizations in the paragraphs below) also set up different special committees, including: Committee for Management of the Churches, Committee for Promoting Self-Reliance, Committee for Research on Self-Development, Committee for Theological Education, Committee for Publishing the Bible,

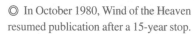

◎ In October 1980, Wind of the Heaven resumed publication after a 15-year stop.

Committee for Publication of Christian Works, Committee for Christian Music, Committee for Women's Affairs and Committee for Ethnic Affairs, etc. Led by the two organizations, all the committees carried out a series of works to promote the construction of the churches in an all-round manner. For instance, based on their actual needs, the Committee for Publishing the Bible printed more than 30 million Bibles in different versions by the end of 2002, including the Old Testament and New Testament in both the simplified Chinese writing style and the original writing style. To provide convenience to ethnic minorities, Bibles in their languages were also published. Besides, to meet Christians' needs of reading an English Bible, it also published Chinese-English Cross-Reference Bibles and Bible Encyclopedias, etc. Wind of Heaven is a magazine published by the two organizations, and since it resumed publication in the summer of 1980, its circulation has been on the rise year after year, becoming a monthly in 1985. While publicizing the three-self patriotic movement, it also carries

articles on such subjects as religious training and how to operate churches well. It often reports and analyzes the important or hot issues in Christian circle, and carries plain but moving stories of Christian life in order to inspire people's love. By 2001, its circulation had reached about 100,000. The publication work of the churches has also

◎ The different versions of Bible and reference books.

◎ Bible in different ethnic languages.

made great progress. The circulation of Hymn (the New Edition) had reached over 10 million, a quarter of which were works by Chinese Christians. Besides, many Bible tapes, Bible poetry selections, and books about Christian theology, history and culture were also published, which included works written by Chinese Christians, translations of the European and American works, and books by theologists from Taiwan, Hong Kong and other places. These publications meet needs of Christians at different levels and were well received.

Great achievements have been accomplished since the three-self patriotic movement was launched in the 1950s. It has become a new task for the Chinese churches concerning how to adhere

◎ Hymn (the New Edition) was published in 1983.

◎ Wind of Heaven and some of the other books published by the two organizations of the Chinese Christian Churches.

to the guideline of the three-self patriotic movement and how to operate under the new social circumstances. The Work Report of the Fourth National Conference of the Chinese Christian Churches pointed out that 'our work concerning three-self is not only self-rule, self-reliance and self-development, but also how to do them well. We should be aware that we are far from the realization of the task of running churches well under the three-self principle. To be frank, we are just standing at the very beginning of the task and the way ahead is still long and rugged'. And the fifth national conference in 1990 clearly put forward that 'we should run churches well under the three-self principle'.

The detailed contents of running churches well by adhering to the three-self principle included: upholding the principle of acting independently and relying on ourselves, encouraging love for Christianity and the country, trying to promote unity and vigorously putting the 'three-good' policy into effect, etc.

Upholding the principle of acting independently and relying on ourselves. China's constitution defined that 'religious groups and affairs allow no domination by the foreign forces'. The three-self patriotic movement launched in 1950 had severed the connections between the Chinese Churches and imperialist

◎ In March 1954, the China Christian Independence Church held the first national conference in Shanghai.

countries, removed the Foreign Missions' rein over them, and achieved self-rule, self-reliance and self-development. In a time when the policy of reform and opening up to the outside world is being implemented, the constitution should still be observed and the three-self principle should still be upheld, so as to fight against the infiltration of overseas anti-China forces, just like what Bishop Ding Guangxun said: 'The routine affairs and the missionary work in the Chinese Churches are matters of our own. Without authorization of the Chinese Churches, no foreigner is allowed to carry out missionary activities in any form in the country.' However, emphasizing independence does not mean total isolation. Friendly exchanges between the Chinese and foreign churches will continue to develop. What the Chinese churches protest against are activities of some foreign churches to split the Chinese churches and regain control over them in the name of spreading evangelism.'

Encouraging love for Christianity and the country. One of the greatest achievements of the three-self patriotic movement is that Chinese Christianity was turned into a religious undertaking operated solely by the Chinese Christians themselves. Loving Christianity and the country has become a faith and a conduct pursued by the masses of Chinese Christians.

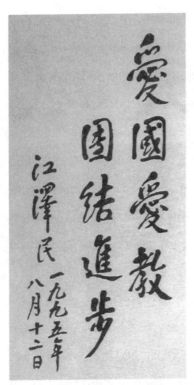

◎ In 1995, the then China's chairman Jiang Zemin wrote to Christian circles, " love the country and Christianity, be united and forge ahead".

China is a socialist country and most of the people do not believe in Christianity, but China is also a country advocating freedom of religious belief. The principle of the CPC in dealing with issues related to religion is: 'the churches shall be politically united and co-operative and respect each other in faith'. Christianity should put less emphasis on the differences between 'believe and not believe' or between 'theism and atheism', and break through the illiberal thinking of only caring for oneself. The churches should also carry forward the Christian virtues and the tradition of serving society, and devote themselves to the construction of the socialist spiritual civilization.

Trying to promote unity. The three-self patriotic movement eliminated the past phenomenon that the Chinese Churches were divided into different factions and the different factions attacked each other. In 1958, the 'united Christian service' was achieved, and China's Christian Churches entered the 'post-factionalism age'. To further promote unity, we advocated the following concepts to operate the churches well through joint efforts: seeking common ground while maintaining differences, respecting each other, and the majority caring more about the minority while the minority considering more about the overall situation. The three-self patriotic movement also insisted on properly handling the relations between the Christians and non-Christians as well as the relations among different Christian factions, treating compatriots with love and strengthening unity among all people.

Vigorously putting the 'three-good' policy into effect. The three-good policy, namely doing a good job in self-rule, doing a good job in self-reliance and doing a good job in self-development, is a further advancement and deepening of the three-self policy. Directed against the current problems in the Churches, this policy raised different requirements in terms of different aspects. As for self-rule, it required the perfection of and earnest obedience to the management system, and the strengthening of democracy and supervision. As for self-reliance, considering China was still economically underdeveloped, the policy advocated the Churches to be thrifty and do what their strength allowed, and reminded them not to expect too much from foreign Church 'support'. Churches in rich areas should help those in poor areas on the basis that the latter must work arduously to try to live on their own. As for self-development, the policy encouraged the churches to disseminate purified evangelism, deepen their knowledge and understanding of Christianity, stand out against heresies, and ponder theological problems in the light of the current situation of China, so as to integrate Christianity with Chinese culture, society and times.

3. *Running well All Kinds of Theological Schools and Fostering Young Priests*

Owing to the influence of the Culture Revolution and the great increase in the number of Christians since the 1980s, China faced a severe short of Christian clergy. In Shanghai, for example, there

◎ In January 1999, Jinling Concord Theological College engaged an overseas theologist as its honorary professor for the first time. The theologist was minister Hong Guangliang (the second on the left), who graduated from Jinling Concord Theological College in the 1950s.

◎ The new teaching building of Zhejiang Theological College was put into use in the spring of 2000.

were about 43,000 Christians and 808 priests in 1949, with each priest responsible for some 54 Christians on average; in 1995, the number of Christians had exceeded 120,000, but there were only 221 priests, with each priest responsible for 540 Christians. To make things worse, many priests had become quite aged and weak and were not able to carry out their work. However, compared with that in other places, the situation in Shanghai was not bad. There were even less priests in rural areas. In some places, one priest had to be responsible for thousands of Christians as well as several churches and gathering places. The worst situation was that some places did not have even one priest, leaving all Christian activities taking place spontaneously, which triggered the boom in heresy and twisted the image of Christianity. To train more priests, Nanjing Jinlin College of Theology reopened and began to recruit students in 1981. This college was established by the National Committee of Three-Self Patriotic Movement of the Protestant Church in China in November 1952, and was constituted of 12 theological schools in eastern China. Bishop Ding Guangxun was its dean. The college stopped classes from 1966 to 1980 due to the impact of the Cultural Revolution,

◎ In the summer of 1996, the graduates of Jinling Concord Theological College were accorded bachelor's degree or master's degree, which was the first time after the Cultural Revolution.

and resumed in February 1981. It provided a four-year regular college program, a three-year postgraduate program and a three-year Bible correspondence program. In addition to the normal science and arts courses, the college also offered theological courses that could be classified in four categories: Bible Research, History of the Churches, Theological Research and Theological Practice. The college took it as a teaching principle to lay emphasis on students' study and self-training with the former playing a major role, and to encourage students to attach importance to self-training by taking part in various kinds of activities held by the churches so as to apply their learning in practice. At present, the college has 27 full-time teachers and 186 students coming from churches all over the country (157 undergraduates and 29 postgraduates). In the 50 years since it was founded, the college has fostered many qualified priests and researchers who stick to the three-self principle and have a relatively high command of theology. Besides this college, many other theological colleges have been established around China. By 1996, there were 17 of these, with Nanjing Jinlin College of Theology at the core and the rest located respectively in Shanghai, Beijing, Chengdu, Wuhan, Shenyang, Fuzhou, Hangzhou, Xi'an, Changsha, Nanchang, Kunming, Zhenzhou, Jinan, Hefei,

◎ Sun Yanli, dean of Shanghai East China Theological College and minister in Shanghai Huai En Church, was discussing religious ethical issues.

Guangzhou and Huhhot. Since the 1980s, China has trained 2,748 students majoring in theology, including 58 postgraduates, 883 undergraduates and 1,807 professional trainees. Currently, there are 1,283 students still studying at school. Some outstanding students were selected to go abroad for advanced studies. Some of them returned and became the backbone of the teaching staff of various theological schools, the leaders of the two organizations at central and local levels, or priests who provide Christian services at grassroots churches.

However, churches in rural areas still face more difficulties than those in urban cities. Christians in rural areas usually were not qualified in terms of theology and were vulnerable to the influence of heresy. To consolidate the rural churches and meet the lack of clergy, the churches developed many kinds of short-term training classes, correspondence courses and professional training classes. By November 2002, more than 50 provincial training centers had been established. The clergy trained in the professional classes, totaling 500,000, have become leaders of the rural churches and have taken the responsibility of managing them and enlightening Christian believers.

4. Actively Promoting the Construction of Theological Ideologies

Theological ideology is the theoretical base for operating churches well under the three-self principle. Chinese Christian theology duplicated Western theology in the 19th and early 20th century, which had many conservative and negative factors. Some cynical, illiberal, irrational and anti-humanity theological ideologies were quite 'marketable' in China, but they were not in accordance with China's situation and culture, and were not suitable for a modern society. The construction of theology was not to negate the basic belief, which is the norm of Christianity and should not be changed. However, in its long development, the Christian churches have made many adaptations to suit the environment in different times, different situations and different countries. These adaptations did not affect the basic beliefs. On the contrary, they made Christian churches more prosperous. The construction of the Chinese theology aimed at expounding the basic belief of Christianity in the light of China's situation and

◎ Minister Shen Cheng'en ordained a new priest for a church of Yi nationality in Yunnan Province in 1982.

culture. It is the certain requirement of the three-self principle, and is a very important element for self-development. As far back as 1956, the Christian magazine Wind of Heaven had launched a mass discussion on theology that were of the utmost concern to Christians, for example, how to perceive and treat the world and its people. Many priests, teachers and students in theological colleges and Christian believers actively joined the discussion and contributed their opinions. In the 1980s and 1990s, since the Churches were busy carrying out State policies by restoring organizations and reopening churches, they were unable to give enough attention to the construction of theology, leading to ideas that were unsuitable for the age and the society. In the late 1990s, theological construction was put on the agenda. The two organizations made the decision to 'strengthen theological construction' at the Jinan Conference held in 1998, which was warmly welcomed by the mass of clergymen and Christian believers.

Bishop Ding Guangxun attached great significance to this work. He stated that 'theology is the thinking of the churches', and that 'a religion that disregards theology is a junior and primitive religion and must be out of tune with reason. The theological thinking advocated by Bishop Ding is about how to combine Christian belief with the reality to form a theory that is both rational and transcendent. He contended that Chinese churches ought to have their own theology. He put forward many positive ideas that were mainly collected in the book entitled Collected Works of Ding Guangxun published in 1998. This contained 82 pf the bishop's speeches or articles, which can be divided into five parts according to their contents, namely speeches abroad, Christian theology, the three-self principle and operation of churches, religious policy and religious research, and remembrances and wishes, in which more than half are related to Christian theology. In this book, Bishop Ding set forth many creative breakthroughs on some fundamental theological issues. for instance, as for the outlook of God, he proposed that Chinese Christians should 'abandon a revengeful, frightening and dictatorial God', but accept a 'God of love'. He thought the most essential character of God was love, and God's love permeated the entire human world and universe. This ideology was in line with the traditional Chinese culture and made Christianity more acceptable to the Chinese people. As for the theory of Jesus Christ, he claimed that 'Jesus belongs to the universe', and that 'Jesus' rule, care, and love pervade the entire universe'. He thought the creation, maintenance, redemption, perfection and the end of universe was a whole process, in which God engaged himself via Jesus, so that all of the virtues in the world were of Jesus' concern and all matters created by God were protected by Jesus. Christians should be more modest and forgiving, and care for people and society with love. As for humanity, while the traditional Christian Churches stress people's sins and are inclined to negate people's value, Bishop Ding, after having assimilated the traditional Chinese ideology of 'human nature is good', contended that 'human beings were created by God according to his own profile' and 'were semi-finished work'. He not only pointed out the necessity of redemption, but also emphasized

◎ A meeting on the publication of Collected Works of Ding Guangxun was held in Beijing in 1998.

the moral duty of human beings as well as their potential for development. Besides, he gave his own answers in many of his articles to such problems as how to treat the virtues outside Christianity, and how to treat atheists, etc. The advancement, openness, and tolerance in his thoughts represent a treasure of the Chinese churches.

Currently, the construction of Christian theology has drawn the attention of many priests and Christians. Theological symposiums and discussions have been held in many places to exchange views and opinions, which had greatly expanded their knowledge and understanding in this regard. Many clergymen

◎ Bishop Ding Guangxun went to Hong Kong to attend a ceremony in which he congratulated Kuang Guangjie on his promotion as the ever first archbishop of Hong Kong Anglican Churches.

thought it was the best period for the development of Chinese Christianity now, and the most urgent question during this period was how to adapt the theology to current conditions when facing the social climate of reform and opening up to the outside world. They thought theological discussion was not only a means to adapt the churches to society so that evangelism could be spread in a better way, but also an important approach to operating the churches well in the three-self principle. The discussion was required by the current situation and the clergymen themselves. Many clergymen also maintained that the theological base of the Chinese churches was relatively weak and clergy quality was not high overall. Consequently, on the one hand, they were not able to guide the beliefs of those intellectual Christians in urban cities who had broad knowledge, and on the other hand, neither could they lead those Christians in rural places who had been deeply poisoned by superstition or passive ideologies due to distorted faith. The quality of the Chinese clergy must be improved and the theology with Chinese characteristics must be established before the churches can obtain a footing in open society and in the churches of the world. The theological construction was neither decided by an individual's disposition, nor inflicted by the government or a senior official, but was an

◎ In November 1999, a symposium about the theological ideologies of the teachers of the Christian training classes was held in Nanjing.

inevitable stage that the Chinese Churches must go though. Everyone in Christian circles should pay sufficient attention in this regard and actively participate in these efforts. Some symposiums held discussions on problems that were of common concern of the churches, such as how to handle the relationship between the churches and society, between faith and reason, how to treat material property, and how to help Christian believers to face ethics, etc. These symposiums achieved sound effects.

Since the launch of the construction of theological ideologies, Chinese Churches have evolved a fashion of studying, thinking and discussing, in which Christians in different places, at different ages or with different experiences can exchange views and learn from each other. And this fashion has pushed forward the development of the construction. Bishop Ding remarked: 'I hope after a long period of development, a new Chinese Christianity with reason, intelligence and sense of justice can rise on the oriental horizon. It will hold firm Jesus Christ and morality, and present us with a loving and beautiful God, not a tyrannical one. Chinese Christianity will bring to the whole world a significant signal.

5. Carrying out Public Welfare Undertakings and Social Service Activities

Christianity is a religion stressing love and dedication. Taking Jesus as their model, the broad masses of Chinese Christians, led by the Churches at various levels, have been actively devoted to the spiritual construction of society. They are dedicated to carrying on the positive spirit in Christian ethics and serving society as well as the people.

In the 20 years since 1978 when the policy of reform and opening up to the outside world was adopted, the Chinese churches did much work to serve society. Churches at different levels mobilized believers to devote themselves to public service activities, led and organized them to do good deeds for the people, for instance, building roads and bridges, helping poverty-stricken people and providing medical services, etc. Through such service, Christians were better involved in society and the social profile of Christianity further improved. In Chuanshi Island in Fujian Province, there was a group of PLA (People's Liberation Army)

◎ The two organizations of Beijing Municipality donated a primary school to Zhoukoudian, a suburb location of Beijing.

soldiers safeguarding the border. These soldiers were busy with their everyday training and work, thus did not have time to take care of their own lives. To make things worse, limited water and inconvenient transportation posed a big challenge, especially in washing clothes. Then, eight Christian fisherwomen voluntarily formed a group to help the soldiers. They gave up their leisure time every Saturday and Sunday, got to the garrison in the early morning, and washed and mended the soldiers' clothes, shoes, socks, quilts, etc. Hot summer or cold winter, they never stopped. Their actions deeply moved the soldiers and a tight friendly relationship between them and the Christians was established. Later, when the Christians were short of labor in building their church, the PLA soldiers automatically came to their help, as embodied in their 'fish and water' relationship. The eight fisherwomen received church awards many times, and the church was also praised by the provincial government and the military as an excellent organization in socialist spiritual construction.

In recent years, owning to industrial restructuring, there appeared many laid-off workers in many cities, mainly middle-aged women in their 30s or 40s. It has become a major issue for the government and society with regard to how to help them get re-employed. The National Association of Young Men's Christian Association established a foreign-related family service college, which was the first of its kind in Shanghai, offering training services to the laid-off women for free. The college not only taught skills of cooking, ikebana, washing and ironing, but also offered such lessons as 'The Role, Status and Professional Ethics of Housework Managers', 'Foreign Culture, Custom and Etiquette', 'Employer Psychology', English, etc. 'Employer Psychology' was even taught by a foreigner. Many laid-off women became foreign-related nurses after the training, and saw their own value in the work, so that they were able to regain their courage as well as confidence in life. The college also offered many training programs on economic courses like commerce, taxation, etc, so as to help more people obtain the necessary skills for survival in modern society.

In China, many places have entered the period of an aged society, and the issue of elderly people has become an outstanding problem. Many Christian churches established various kinds of homes or apartments for the aged to help those feeling lonely or sick to enjoy their lives. Compared with those in foreign countries, the homes for the aged established by the Chinese churches were simple and crude, but the love offered by the managers and attendants was not disappointing. They not only satisfied the

◎ The elderly people in the Sheng Ai Home for the Aged that was sponsored by the church in Wuhu City, Anhui Province were enjoying the New Year's Eve together.

material needs of the elderly people in their daily lives, but also held activities like choral singing or dialogues to maintain their mental health. And the attendants also gave special treatment to those who could not take care of themselves. Limited by the actual financial situation of the Chinese Churches, some homes for the elderly people invented a lot of special ways of nursing. Take the 'Apartment for the Aged' in Hangzhou as an example, it implemented the 'ladder service' model, in which the relatively 'young' old people who were about 60 years old were expected to attend to those who were sick and could not take care of themselves. By this means, it was not only conducive to the establishment of harmonious relations among the elderly people; in addition, it solved the problem of insufficiency of human and financial resources. With this model handed on from generation after generation, the old people who offer their love today will surely be rewarded in the future.

From the 1980s to the end of 1990s, a series of natural disasters occurred in China, like floods in northeast China, earthquake in Yunnan Province, forest fires, and especially the flood in 1998 which endangered more than 10 provinces and municipalities and was quite unusual in Chinese history. People throughout the nation, including Christians, were most concerned

◎ The two organizations of Shanghai Municipality donated 200,000 Yuan for the earthquake-stricken people in Taiwan in October 1999.

about those living in the flood-stricken area and made many donations. In an evening event sponsored by CCTV (China Central Television), the two church organizations donated 1 million Yuan ($120,000). Besides, the Amity Foundation initiated by Christians donated 10 million Yuan ($1.2 million); Shanghai Christians raised 500,000 Yuan or $60,000 for the Shanghai Municipal Red Cross. The Christian churches in different places launched many activities to mobilize funds for the stricken people, and many Christians voluntarily donated their clothes to the churches, and these were gathered and transported to the flood-stricken areas. Besides donations, the Christians also actively took part in the struggle against the flood. In Jiayu County, Hubei

Province, which was seriously inundated, the local church opened its doors and accommodated more than 300 homeless refugees. Charity donation has become a prominent tradition of the Chinese Christian Churches. In recent years, and the beneficiaries include the China Welfare Foundation for the Disabled, Shanghai Children's Welfare House, etc.

Among all the Chinese Christian organizations engaged in social services, the Amity Foundation established in April 1985 has been one of the most prominent. It is a non-governmental organization initiated by some Chinese Christians with the help and support from people of different industries as well as overseas Christians, and mainly engaged in charity work and such social

◎ The Amity Foundation donated books to primary and secondary schools in Zhijiang County, Hunan Province.

© The Amity Hospital established by the churches in Linqu County, Shangdong Province was known far and wide.

services as medicine, education, social welfare in rural areas. It became a new approach for Chinese Christians to join their efforts in social services. Between 1995 and 1996, the Amity Foundation collected more than 30 million Yuan (about $3.7 million), and contributed all the funds to society, of which nearly 20 million Yuan (about $2.4 million) was invested in medical services in rural areas and disaster relief. The work of the Amity Foundation was not simply poverty relief or to solve material difficulties, but to help the poor regions improve the production, education and healthcare system through its services, so as to enhance people's living standards. During the process of offering help, the Churches kept close co-operation with the local government and people, and strengthened church ties with society. For example, Fan village in Henan Province was in great need of water, lack of which had gravely hindered its development and had posed a threat to the livelihood of the villagers, leaving more than 4,000 households and 20,000 people in poverty for decades. But lack of funds held up the launch of a planned large-scale drawing water project. The local Church informed the Amity Foundation of the problem and it immediately input over 2 million Yuan ($240,000). The project started as it had been planned and was completed successfully. The water problem that had been annoying the village for a long time was eventually resolved. The villagers were very thankful for the financial support, and the Church and the Amity Foundation also realized their value in this process. The Amity Foundation focused its services in the poverty-stricken areas and ethnic minority areas scattered mainly in the central and western parts of China by investing in projects

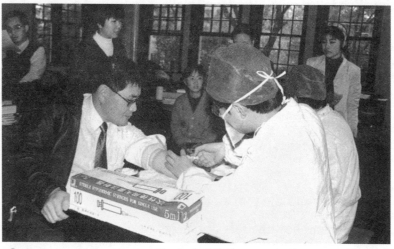

◎ Students in Jinling Concord Theological College donate blood.

for the comprehensive development of the rural areas to help people out of poverty as soon as possible. They also offered technical and English training programs, as well as healthcare programs. Besides, they provided financial aid to children who had dropped study for poverty for them to go back to school. In 2001, the Amity Foundation accomplished more than 10,000 cataract extraction operations in Ningxia, Gansu and Hubei provinces and trained thousands of doctors and nurses for the counties, towns and villages there. It also invested about 350 million Yuan or $40 million in publicity on AIDS prevention and community care programs in five counties in Yunnan Province, where 1.14 million people enjoyed benefits. In addition, it collaborated with the China Health Education Association to make videodiscs about AIDS, and sent more than 10 thousand copies free to the concerned departments. Since its establishment, the Amity Foundation has attracted much attention from the Christian churches all over the world, including the World Christian Churches (WCC), which also conveyed its willingness to help.

To expand the range of social services provided by the Chinese churches, the two organizations established a 'Social Service Department' in May 2002, aiming at concentrating their attention, energy, and resources both at home and abroad to contribute more to the poverty-relief program, public services and aid for emergencies. The first project was to donate wheelchairs to the disabled in Zhengzhou, Henan Province, which led some young students from Zhengzhou University to express their willingness to join team of volunteers. The social service work by the Chinese Christian churches has generated quite good social effects.

At present, altogether 45 social service projects are under construction by the churches across the country, ranging from homes for the elderly, kindergartens, clinics, health center for disabled children and aid for poor school-aged children to enter school, etc. The local churches and two organizations in various places are trying hard to do a good job in their social service work by caring for the disadvantaged social groups and carrying out charity and public activities. Although they have just started their efforts and their work is still on the initial stage and on a small scale, the Chinese churches have demonstrated their fledgling vigor. They will strive in line with what was put forward by the seventh National Conference of the Chinese Christianity to 'continue to serve the society and the people and act as a witness for the goodness of Christianity'.

6. Strengthening the Friendly Exchanges with Christian Churches around the World

Christianity is a universal religion, and Chinese Christianity is one part of it. Based on respecting each other's sovereignty and on the basis of equality, amity and mutual respect, the Chinese Christian churches attach great importance to exchanges with overseas churches and Christians, as well as the maintenance of

◎ The Chinese Christian Delegation visited the U.K. in October 1982.

good relations with them. Since the 1980s, the Chinese churches have stepped up communications with others in the world, and have been trying hard to get involved in the world Christian community. The China Christian

◎ On 24 December 1985, Jinling Concord Theological College and Jinling Hotel jointed efforts and held a large-scale Christmas concert in Nanjing City. Altogether over 600 people celebrated this event on the Christmas Eve, including foreign students, teachers, experts and travelers from more than ten countries, the Hong Kong and Macao compatriots as well as faculty of Jinling Concord Theological College.

Council formally participated in WCC in February 1991, and consequently tightened its exchanges with world Christianity. In the five years between 1991 and 1996, the two Christian organizations of China sent altogether 108 delegations to over 30 countries and regions, selectively attended many international Christian conferences held abroad, and received 203 visiting Christian delegations, including many delegations led by the world class Christian leaders like the then Archbishop of Canterbury George Carey and his predecessor Robert Runcie, World Council of Churches General Secretary Dr. Konrad Raiser, and the chairman and general secretary of World Association of

Lutherans, etc. In the five years between 1997 and 2002, the two organizations altogether received 261 Christian delegations and 3,301 person-times from different countries and regions around the world, including the U.S. religious leaders delegation invited by then Chinese president Jiang Zemin, a Lutheran delegation from Finland, an Anglican delegation from Australia, etc. While continuing the exchanges with the U.S. and European Churches, the two organizations also strengthened their ties with churches in South Korea, Japan, Singapore, Malaysia and other neighboring countries. Besides, the two organizations also sent many delegations abroad, for example, in the year 2000, Han Wenzao and Cao Shengjie, respectively chairman and vice-chairman of the two organizations, participated in the Millennium World Peace Summit of Religious and Spiritual Leaders held in the U.N. headquarters in New York as representatives from China, which demonstrated the Chinese Christians' longing for world peace. In June 2002, Cao Shengjie led a Chinese Christian delegation to participated in the Asian Conference on Religion and Peace held in Indonesia, and Deng Fucun led a delegation to participate in the World Council of Religious and Spiritual Leaders held in Thailand. In these religious conferences, the Chinese Christian leaders called on the religious people in the

◎ The U.S. religious leaders delegation joined hands with the Chinese Christian leaders in February 1998.

world to promote the communications between different religions and cultures, so as to deepen their mutual understanding and to seek the unity and harmony in the process of religious diversification.

In the exchanges of the Chinese Christian churches with those of other countries and regions, as well as their exchanges with other religions, they have been concentrating on appealing for justice and peace and maintaining the interests of the country. On the one hand, they actively develop their relations with the churches and people of other countries; on the other hand, they oppose and refute the Western anti-China forces' calumny and attacks on China's religious issues. In September 2000, directed against Vatican's distortion of history and motive of canonization, the two organizations timely published 'An Announcement of Opposition to Vatican's Distortion of History and Motive of Canonization'. Directed against some Western countries that attacked China in the excuse of religious and human rights issues, the major directors of the two organizations also led many delegations to the U.S., Switzerland and other countries and met the Christian people as well as media there to clarify the truth and voice our own opinions, which strongly refuted the attacks and produced sound effects.

China has participated in WTO, and will open to the world in an all round way. Therefore, the friendly exchanges between the Chinese and overseas churches will surely becoming more and more frequent. The Chinese churches need the world, and the world churches need China. During their exchanges with the overseas churches, the principle of independence will always maintain at the core to the Chinese churches, in which they will carry on their cooperation and communication in the new century.

图书在版编目（CIP）数据

中国基督教／罗伟虹著．—北京：五洲传播出版社，2004.6

（中国宗教基本情况丛书）

ISBN 7-5085-0534-4

Ⅰ．中...　Ⅱ．罗...　Ⅲ．基督教史－中国－英文　Ⅳ．B979.2

中国版本图书馆 CIP 数据核字（2004）第 050987 号

《中国基督教》

责任编辑：荆孝敏

编辑助理：蔡　程

图片提供：罗伟虹　新华社摄影部等

设计承制：北京紫航文化艺术有限公司

翻　译：朱承铭

《中国基督教》

五洲传播出版社

地址：中国北京北三环中路31号　邮编：100088

电话：82008174　网址：www.cicc.org.cn

开本：140×210　1/32　印张：5.5

2004 年 6 月第一版　印数 1-7000

ISBN 7-5085-0534-4/B·41

定价：48.00元